MW00574522

Music Theory

for Bass Players

by Steve Gorenberg

PLAYBACK+
Speed • Pitch • Balance • Loop

To access audio and video visit:
www.halleonard.com/mylibrary

Enter Code
4950-0301-2040-8672

ISBN: 978-1-4950-7571-1

HAL•LEONARD®

Visit Hal Leonard Online at
www.halleonard.com

Contact Us:
Hal Leonard
7777 West Bluemound Road
Milwaukee, WI 53213
Email: info@halleonard.com

In Europe contact:
Hal Leonard Europe Limited
Distribution Centre, Newmarket Road
Bury St Edmunds, Suffolk, IP33 3YB
Email: info@halleonardeurope.com

In Australia contact:
Hal Leonard Australia Pty. Ltd.
4 Lentara Court
Cheltenham, Victoria, 3192 Australia
Email: info@halleonard.com.au

Contents

Introduction

Welcome to *Music Theory for Bass Players*. This book covers all of the essential elements of music theory, from the very basics to complex scales and chords. Understanding music theory can prove to be an overwhelming mystery for many beginners, but we've used diagrams and tablature (tab) to present the majority of the material, as it directly relates to the fretboard. You won't need to have a lot of experience reading music notation, although music notation has been included throughout. We'll tackle the concepts of theory gradually, and the information should be helpful for players of all levels. The goal is to get you to visualize intervals, arpeggios, scales, and chord progressions directly on the fretboard as they apply specifically to playing bass.

Throughout the book, we'll cover topics such as memorizing the notes on the fretboard, major and minor scales, pentatonic scales, arpeggios, intervals, chord progressions, modes, and complex scales, all with a focus on how to apply them to your playing. We'll take a look at the bass styles of some of the masters and use theory to analyze and understand their approach to constructing bass lines. There's also a section at the end with backing tracks for you to jam along with and apply what you've learned. For many of the chapters, we've included reviews, quizzes, and tips to help reinforce what you've learned as you progress.

We'll cover the material at a pace that's gradual enough for beginners with limited playing experience, making this book a great companion to their regular curriculum while they're learning how to play the instrument. Intermediate and advanced players who already have some music theory background will also gain a fresh perspective on how to apply the concepts directly to the fretboard. Rather than overwhelming you with a lot of complex theory that's useful for jazz guitarists or keyboard players, we'll focus on the elements that are essential for the bass player, like how to write bass lines, how to lay down a solid foundation, and how to improvise.

Each new section will be built upon concepts covered in previous chapters, so take your time and be sure you have a good understanding of the material before jumping ahead. Grab your bass and let's get started!

About the Audio & Video

Audio tracks accompany the lessons so you can hear what each example sounds like. Backing tracks are also provided so you can jam along. Plus three bonus video lessons on bass fretboard theory are included! To access all of the audio tracks and videos that accompany this book, simply go to **www.halleonard.com/mylibrary** and enter the code found on page 1. The examples that include audio are marked with the 🔊 symbol throughout the book.

About the Author

Steve Gorenberg is a bass player, music educator, author, arranger, transcriber, and music engraver based in Los Angeles. Steve started out at Cherry Lane Music's print division as a transcriber and in-house music editor. He has since continued as a freelance transcriber, editor, and engraver for Cherry Lane Music, *Guitar for the Practicing Musician* magazine, Hal Leonard, Fred Russell Publishing, and Warner Bros. Inc., and has written, edited, and designed numerous music education products, including *Warm-Up Exercises for Bass Guitar*, *100 Rock Bass Lessons*, *How to Create Rock Bass Lines*, and *Teach Yourself to Play Guitar Chords*. To date, Steve has created thousands of official note-for-note guitar and bass transcriptions for artists, including Metallica, Guns N' Roses, the Red Hot Chili Peppers, the Rolling Stones, Van Halen, Pearl Jam, Rush, Black Sabbath, Queen, and John Mayer.

Chapter 1: The Musical Alphabet

Let's start at the very beginning: the musical alphabet and first-position notes on the bass. You may already be familiar with the material in this chapter, but it's a good idea to review it all and make sure you know the basic terminology we'll be using throughout this book. All of the examples will be presented with a combination of music notation, tablature, and fretboard diagrams. Although you don't need to read complex musical notation in order to apply the principles of music theory to your playing, it's helpful to be able to identify the basic pitches on a musical staff in bass clef.

THE NOTES IN FIRST POSITION

Memorizing the names of the open strings and the notes in first position will give you a good foundation for understanding the musical alphabet and will make it easier to learn the rest of the notes on the fretboard. Below are the four open-string notes—E, A, D, and G—shown in notation and tablature, with a fretboard diagram on the right. If you can identify these four notes in music notation, you can use them as reference points on the staff to help you find the other notes in the alphabet.

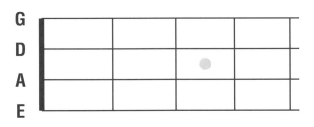

The fretted notes in first position should correspond to each of the four fingers of your fret hand. Fret the notes at the first fret with your index finger, the notes at the second fret with your middle finger, and so on. For now, let's focus on just the *natural notes*—the regular letter-name notes of the musical alphabet that contain no sharps or flats (A, B, C, D, E, F, and G). The natural notes in first position on the fourth string are E, F, and G.

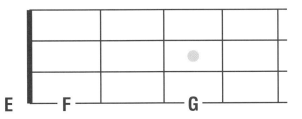

Notice how the notes progress up the staff in order, alternating between lines and spaces. Here are the first-position natural notes on the third string—A, B, and C:

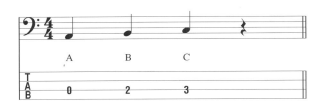
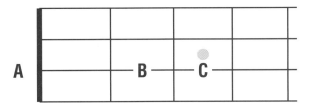

The following two examples utilize the first-position notes on the third and fourth strings. Try saying each note name as you play along with the audio tracks. Make sure your bass is in tune before you begin.

TRACK 1

Moderately

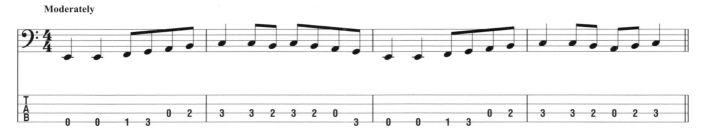

TRACK 2

Moderately

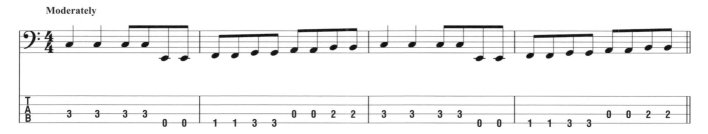

Here are the natural notes in first position on the second string—D, E, and F:

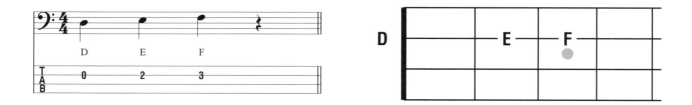

The first-position natural notes on the first string are G, A, and B.

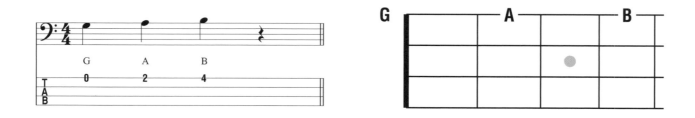

The next two examples are designed to help you memorize the first-position notes on the first and second strings. Say each of the note names aloud as you play along.

TRACK 3

TRACK 4

Here's a simple pattern for practicing the notes in first position on all four strings. Play through it slowly and in time, then gradually increase the speed once you've got the pattern memorized. If you're learning these note names for the first time, make sure you've got them down before proceeding.

TRACK 5

INTERVALS

The distance in pitch between two musical notes is called an *interval*. Generally speaking, music theory, and the way it applies to scales and chords, is based on the study of intervals. An interval is simply a unit of measurement that describes the space between two particular notes—how much higher or lower one note sounds from another. The smallest interval in the musical alphabet is a *half step*. On the bass, a half step is the distance from one fretted note to the fretted note next to it on the same string. In the fretboard diagram below, you can see that the distance between the notes B and C on the third string is one fret. Therefore, the interval from B to C is a half step.

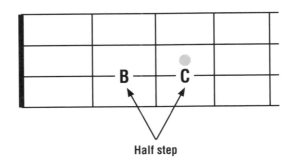

Half step

Using standard musical terminology, it can also be said that the note C is a *half step higher* than the note B, and conversely, the note B is a *half step lower* than the note C.

The other interval used in the musical alphabet is a *whole step*, which is the distance of two frets on the same string. In the diagram below, you can see that the distance between the notes F and G on the fourth string is two frets; therefore, the interval from F to G is a whole step. We can also say that the note G is a *whole step higher* than the note F, and conversely, the note F is a *whole step lower* than the note G.

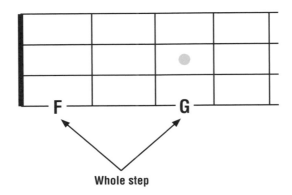

Whole step

Let's take another look at the first-position notes on the bass from open A on the third string to A at the second fret on the first string. The notation below indicates which intervals are half steps (H) and which are whole steps (W). You'll notice that there are half steps between the notes B and C, and the notes E and F. These half steps occur naturally in the musical alphabet. The intervals between all of the other consecutive notes are whole steps.

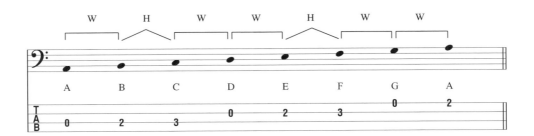

Once you memorize where the natural half steps occur on the fretboard, you'll be equipped with reference points you can use to locate the rest of the natural notes. The example below focuses on the natural half steps in first position (between B and C, and between E and F).

TRACK 6

Moderately

Another important interval worth discussing at this point is the *octave*, which is the distance between two notes with the same letter name; for instance, from the note A to the next higher (or lower) A. The musical alphabet only uses the seven letters A through G, then it starts over again on the next higher A. It can therefore be said that the note A at the second fret of the 1st string is *one octave higher* than the open A on the third string. The following chart shows one octave of the regular letter-name notes from A to A, with the half steps and whole steps indicated.

For each pair of notes that are a whole step apart, there's another fretted note that falls in between them. These notes are indicated using *sharps* and *flats*. A sharp (♯) placed on a note raises its pitch by a half step; a flat (♭) placed on a note lowers its pitch by a half step. In the diagram below, you'll see that the note at the second fret on the fourth string can either be called F♯ or G♭; both names are correct and refer to the exact same pitch. Regardless, it can be said that the note F♯ is *one half step higher* than the note F, while the note G♭ is *one half step lower* than the note G.

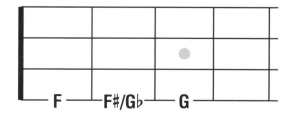

Two notes with different names but have the same exact pitch are referred to as being *enharmonic*. For example, F♯ and G♭ are enharmonic. It can also be said that F♯ is the *enharmonic equivalent* of G♭.

Sharps and flats are the two most common types of *accidentals*. Accidentals are added to regular letter-name notes to alter their pitch. Whether a sharp or flat is used depends on the specific musical context, key, or scale—concepts that we'll explore in the coming chapters. In cases that aren't dependent on the key or scale, sharps will usually be used for ascending passages, and flats will be used for descending passages.

The unaltered letter-name notes (A–B–C–D–E–F–G) are also referred to as *natural notes*. By extension, the half-step or whole-step intervals between them are called *natural half steps* and *natural whole steps*. It can therefore be said that, in the musical alphabet, natural half steps occur between B and C, and between E and F. This phenomenon can best be viewed on a piano keyboard, where all of the notes are consecutive—the white keys are natural notes, and the black keys are notes with accidentals. The diagram below shows one octave of notes on the keyboard from C to C. You can see that the white keys E and F are right next to each other with no black key in between them. This is also true for the white keys B and C.

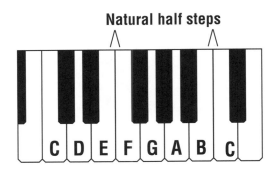

Watch Your Steps

If the information in this chapter is new to you, take the time to review it and make sure you understand the concept of natural half steps, whole steps, and accidentals, and you have a firm grasp of the terminology. This is usually where beginners get confused, but everything moving forward will be based on these concepts. When we talk about intervals and the distance between notes, it's not a visual distance, but a sonic distance that measures how much higher or lower one note is to another, or the distance in *pitch*. At this point, it's best to just memorize that the natural half steps are between B and C, and between E and F—*always*. Many beginners will wonder *why* that is, instead of simply accepting it at face value. Just trust us—it's been that way for a thousand years, when the musical alphabet was first invented. It's based on the physics of soundwaves and lots of other complicated mathematical things that you don't need to know the specifics of right now.

THE CHROMATIC SCALE

If you play a full octave of consecutive half steps, including all of the natural notes and accidentals, you'll have what's called the *chromatic scale*. In addition, playing any passage of notes that progresses in a series of consecutive half steps is referred to as playing *chromatically*. The following example is a one-octave chromatic scale, ascending from the open A on the third string to the A an octave higher on the first string, then descending back to the open A. The notation uses sharps for the ascending part and flats for the descending part.

TRACK 7

Slow

Note: Another type of accidental is the *natural* (♮), as seen in the third measure of the example. Naturals are used to cancel out a sharp or flat and return a note to its natural state. In this case, the natural is functioning as a *courtesy accidental*, canceling out the G♯ from the previous measure. Naturals are most commonly used to cancel out accidentals present in the key signature, or accidentals used earlier in the same measure of music.

Here's a chart of the A chromatic scale, using the notes of the complete musical alphabet; it includes all of the natural notes plus the sharp/flat notes in between them. In total, there are 12 different tones between the lower A and the octave A. Remember: A♯ and B♭ are the same-sounding note with two different names, depending on the musical context. All of the intervals between the consecutive notes are half steps; the natural half steps (B and C, and E and F) are labeled above the chart.

		Natural half step				Natural half step			
A	A♯/B♭	B	C	C♯/D♭	D	D♯/E♭	E	F	F♯/G♭	G	G♯/A♭	A

Here's an example showing how you can create bass riffs with the chromatic scale. Chromatic passages like these are common in many bass lines.

TRACK 8

Moderately

REVIEW QUIZ

Answers are on the bottom of the next page.

1. Name the three natural notes in first position on the fourth string.

2. Name the three natural notes in first position on the second string.

3. In the musical alphabet, which pairs of natural notes are a half step apart?

4. What note is a whole step higher than F?

5. What note is a half step lower than C?

6. Collectively, sharps and flats are known as _____.

7. What note is an octave higher than E?

8. What note is a whole step higher than B?

9. What note is a half step higher than G?

14

Identify the notes in the following fretboard diagrams:

10.

11.

12.

13.

14.

15.

QUICK REVIEW:

- The names of the open strings (lowest to highest) are E, A, D, and G.
- The distance in pitch between two musical notes is called an interval.
- A half step is the distance from one fretted note to the fretted note next to it on the same string.
- A whole step is the distance from one fretted note to the fretted note two frets away from it on the same string.
- In the musical alphabet, natural half steps occur between the notes B and C, and the notes E and F.
- A sharp (♯) placed on a note raises its pitch by a half step; a flat (♭) placed on a note lowers its pitch by a half step.
- A full octave of consecutive half steps is called the chromatic scale.
- In total, there are 12 different tones in the musical alphabet, including all of the natural notes and sharp/flat notes.

Answer Key

1. E, F, and G	6. Accidentals	11. G
2. D, E, and F	7. E	12. B
3. B and C, and E and F	8. C♯ (or D♭)	13. F
4. G	9. G♯ (or A♭)	14. E
5. B	10. A	15. B

Chapter 2: Learning the Fretboard

An important step to mastering the bass is to learn and memorize all of the notes on the fretboard. You should make it your goal to be able to point to any note on the neck and instantly know its name. The key to understanding music theory and making it work for you is learning how to directly apply that information to the bass, and learning the fretboard is essential in that regard. You need to know the language of your own instrument in order to maximize your potential as a player. Memorizing all the notes is a gradual process—and it may seem overwhelming to you at first—but there are shortcuts and recognizable patterns that can give you an advantage and make the task less intimidating and much easier.

UTILIZING THE HALF-STEP AND WHOLE-STEP FORMULA

Using the notes you've already memorized as reference points, you can use the musical alphabet's half-step and whole-step formula to identify any other note on the fretboard. Remember: most of the consecutive natural notes are two frets apart (whole steps), with the exception of B and C, and E and F, which are one fret apart (half steps).

First Position, Chromatically

You should have the first-position natural notes from Chapter 1 memorized by now. Let's add in the sharp and flat notes. The diagram below contains the notes at every fret, and the example that follows presents all of the notes chromatically. As before, we've used sharps while ascending and flats while descending.

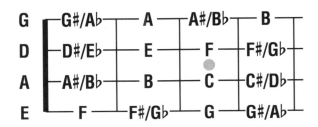

TRACK 9

The Natural Notes on One String

Now it's time to break out of first position and find the natural notes further up the fretboard. Let's plot the notes in a linear fashion on one string by continuing up the fretboard from first position, using the musical alphabet and the half-step and whole-step formula. For the rest of this section, we'll focus on the natural notes; the sharps and flats will be easy to locate once you know where the natural notes are located.

The diagram below shows all the natural notes on the fourth string, up to the 12th fret. Notice that the half steps are located where the notes are only one fret apart—between the open string and first fret (E and F), and between the seventh and eighth frets (B and C),

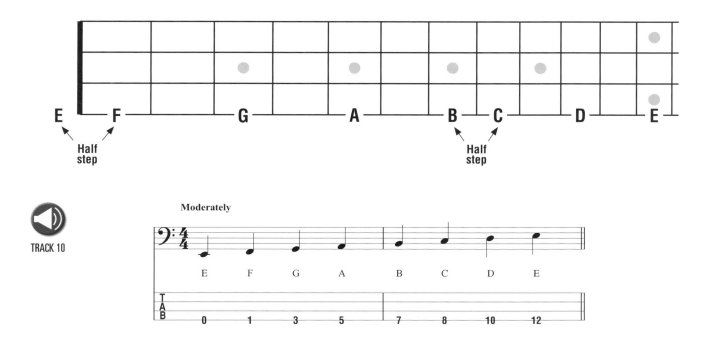

Now let's do the same thing on the third string. Here, the half steps occur between the second and third frets (B and C), and between the seventh and eighth frets (E and F).

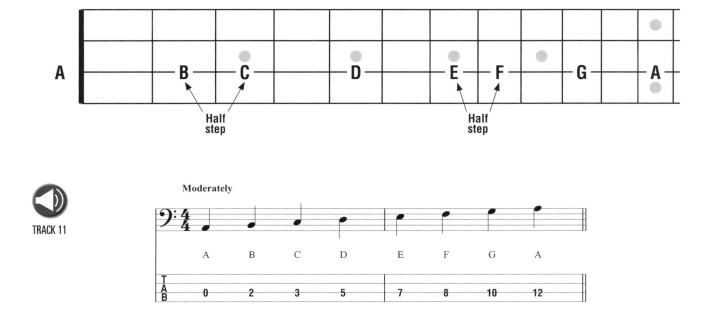

Here's a bass riff to help you memorize the natural notes on strings 3 and 4. Once you have the locations of the notes memorized, feel free to reverse or mix up the order and create your own variations.

TRACK 12

Using the Octave Pattern

Because of the way the bass is tuned, the finger patterns used for playing intervals are consistent, no matter what fret or string you start them on. This makes it easy to transpose scales and arpeggios, but it can also help you to identify the notes on the bass. The octave interval is especially useful for this, and it's also one of the most common intervals played in bass lines. For any note on the third or fourth strings, its octave will always be located two frets and two strings higher. The octave pattern is shown below for notes at the third and fifth frets.

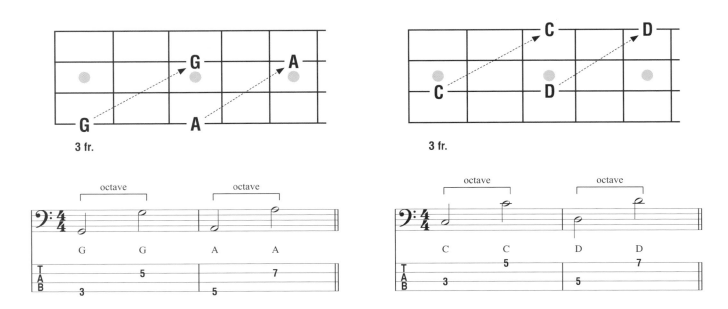

If you were able to memorize the natural notes on the fourth string by using the half-step and whole-step formula on the previous page, you can use the octave pattern to easily locate all of the natural notes on the second string.

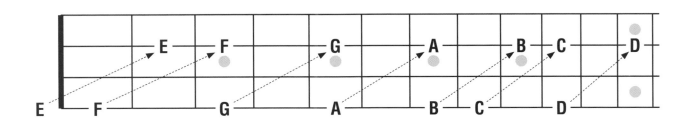

TRACK 13

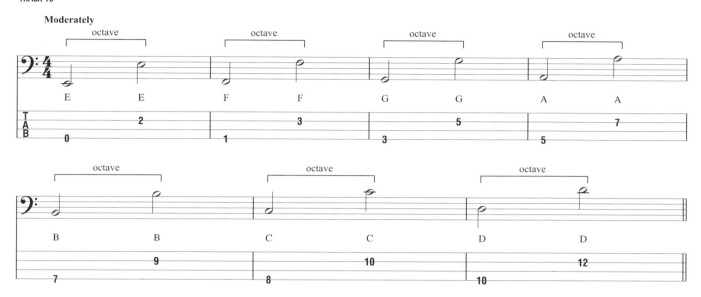

Now let's use the octave pattern and the notes on the third string to identify all of the notes on the first string.

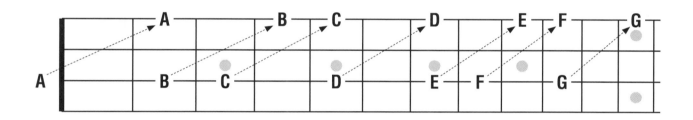

TRACK 14

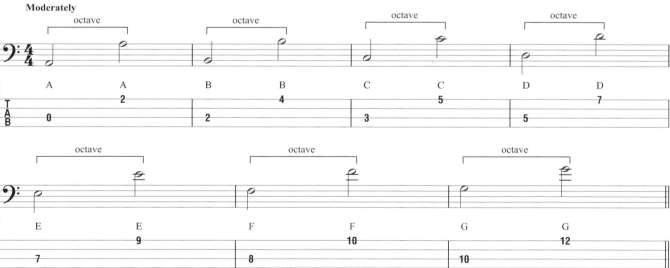

SHORTCUTS AND REFERENCE POINTS

In addition to the octave pattern we just used, there are several other patterns and shortcuts that will help to demystify the fretboard and make learning the notes easier. Once you're armed with all of this information, you should be able to find and recognize many of the notes quickly. The following examples are presented to help you to visualize the fretboard and see connections between the notes that will make learning the note names less intimidating. Ultimately, you'll end up using different combinations of these ideas that work best for you.

The 12th Fret

The double-dot fret marker at the 12th fret indicates the point that is one octave from the open strings; therefore, the note names at the 12th fret are the same as the open strings, one octave higher.

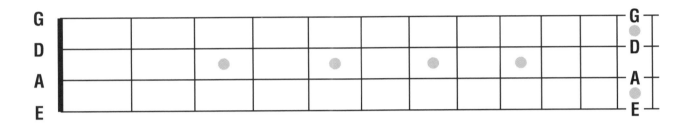

After the 12th fret, the musical alphabet continues as before. The note names at the 13th fret are the same as the note names at the first fret, the note names at the 14th fret are the same as the note names at the second fret, and so on. Here's a diagram and a example featuring the natural notes in 12th position.

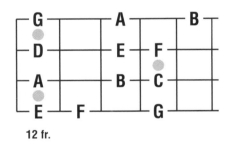

12 fr.

TRACK 15

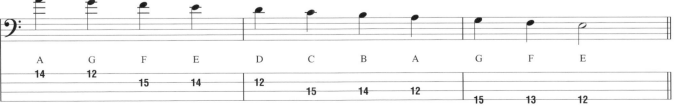

The Fifth Fret

You may already be familiar with the fifth-fret tuning method—each note at the fifth fret is the same pitch as the next higher open string, and you can use this to tune the bass by ear. Using this information, you automatically know the names of the notes at the fifth fret on the second, third, and fourth strings. Let's add in the C note on the first string, which will give us all of the notes at the fifth fret.

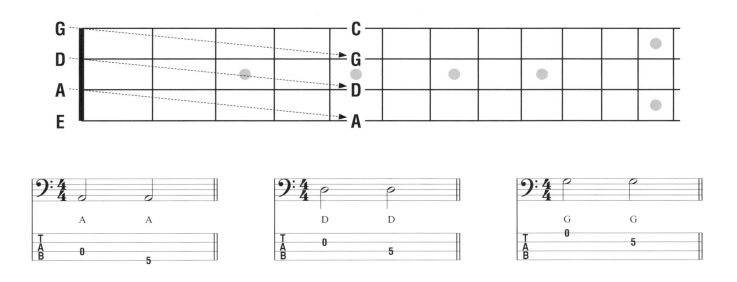

This next bass line is designed to help reinforce the location of the fifth-fret and open-string unison intervals. Even though they're the same pitch, alternating between the open and fretted unison notes can create an interesting effect. We've also incorporated some hammer-ons into the pattern.

TRACK 16

Slow

The Seventh Fret

The next shortcut that you can easily recognize revolves around the notes at the seventh fret. These notes are one octave higher than the open strings below them. You can also use these notes to help you tune the bass by ear. We can include the note B at the seventh fret on the fourth string to complete the set.

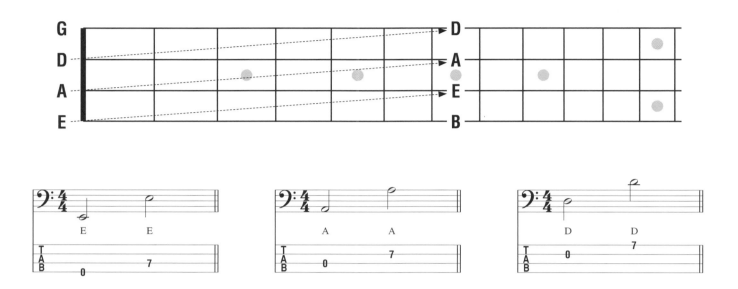

Use of the octave notes at the seventh fret and their open-string counterparts is pretty common in rock and metal bass riffs. Pick players often prefer playing these octaves at the seventh fret since they occur on adjacent strings. Here's a functional bass line that demonstrates this and also incorporates some pull-offs.

TRACK 17

Slow

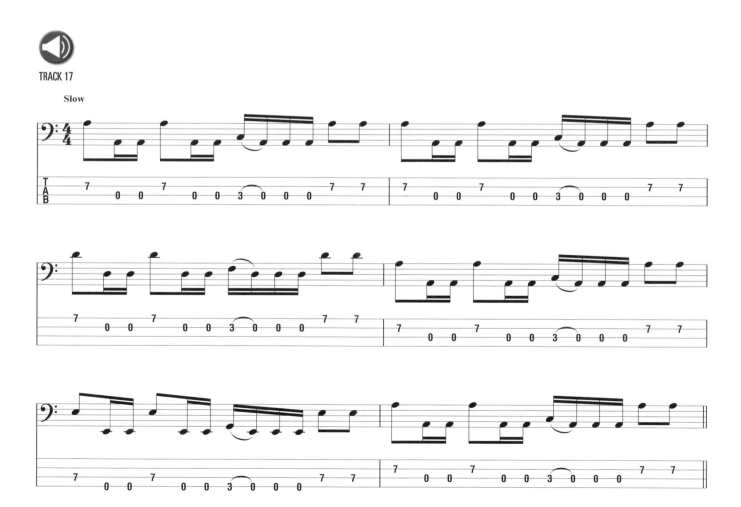

Above the Seventh Fret

So far, we've covered most of the natural notes on the fretboard; the only gap left is the space between the seventh and 12th frets, shown within the dashed box in the following diagram. This will probably be the most difficult area of the neck to remember, but it will come gradually over time.

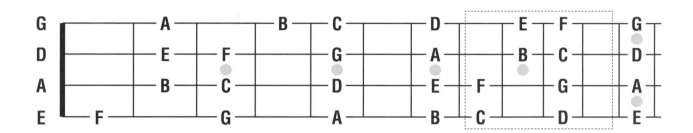

There are a few ways to approach finding the notes. You can use the half-step and whole-step formula to count up from the seventh fret as shown below in the diagram on the left. You can also count backwards in the alphabet from the notes at the 12th fret, shown in the diagram on the right. The natural notes at the 10th fret are all one whole step lower than the notes at the 12th fret.

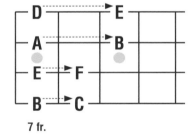

7 fr.

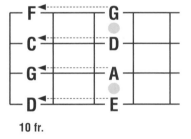

10 fr.

You can also quickly identify some of the notes in this area of the fretboard by using the octave pattern that was presented earlier in the chapter. The diagram on the left shows the notes B and E at the seventh fret with their higher octave notes at the ninth fret. In the diagram on the right, the notes D and G at the 12th fret are shown with their lower-octave counterparts at the 10th fret.

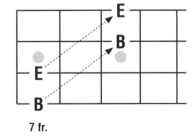

7 fr.

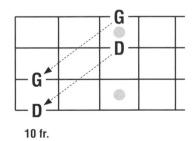

10 fr.

Learn the Fret Markers

The dots on the fretboard are there for your visual reference, so it's extremely helpful to know the notes at these frets. The double-dot at the 12th fret is obviously the octave, and all of the markers higher up the neck from there match with the dots in the lower register, but one octave higher. The notes at the third, fifth, and seventh frets should be easy to remember: the third fret contains the first-position notes we started out with, while the fifth and seventh frets contain the unison and octave notes we discussed earlier that are often used for tuning. The marker at the ninth fret falls within the more obscure part of the fretboard, but it acts as a convenient reference point between the seventh and 12th frets. For simplicity, we've indicated the notes using accidentals at the third and ninth frets by their more commonly used names. Remember: even if you only memorize the notes on the third and fourth strings, you can use the octave pattern to find the notes on the higher strings.

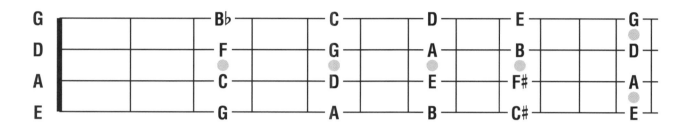

A Gradual Process

You shouldn't come away from this chapter expecting to instantly know where every note on the bass is located. This is a gradual process that can take beginners years to master. In time, you'll be able to point to any fret on any string and know the note immediately. The purpose of this chapter is to help you visualize the fretboard in ways that make it less daunting, and to hopefully get you to memorize some specific, commonly used notes that you can use as reference points. If you're trying to identify a specific note that you don't know, use some of these processes to count forward or backward from the nearest note that you already know. Eventually, you won't need to do this anymore. Remember: the more notes you know on the fretboard, the easier it is to apply music theory, scales, and arpeggios with confidence. You'll also be able to use the bass to help you identify the notes within arpeggios, but more about that later in the book!

BONUS ROUND

The information in this book explores the concepts of music theory as they apply to a regular, four-string bass in standard tuning; however, there are other types of basses and tunings that you'll likely encounter. Let's use the next few pages to take a look at two of these alternatives: the five-string bass and drop D tuning.

Five-String Bass

Use of the five-string bass has increased in popularity in many styles of music. The fourth, third, second, and first strings are identical to a four-string bass (E–A–D–G), but the five-string adds an additional lower string, tuned to a low B. This allows you to play two-and-a-half steps below the standard low E of a four-string bass. The low B is tuned consistently with the rest of the bass, in equal intervals, so all of your patterns, scales, and arpeggios use the same fingerings, and the notes aren't very difficult to identify.

Using the half-step and whole-step formula, we can plot the natural notes on the fifth string, shown below on the fretboard diagram and in notation and tablature.

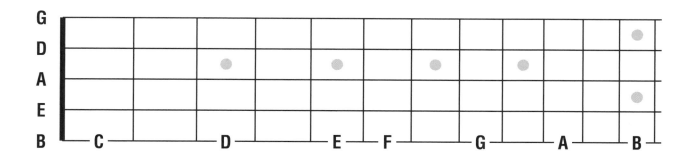

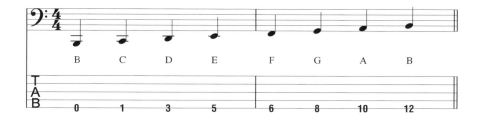

Remembering the open B (as well as the 12th-fret B) is easy. You'll also notice the E at the fifth fret, which you may remember using for the fifth-fret tuning method we discussed earlier. Many players who prefer five-strings often play further up on the neck, above the seventh fret, because you can cover a wider range of notes without moving out of position. For example, something that you might play at the third fret on a four-string bass can be moved up to the eighth fret on a five-string, giving you a whole extra string's worth of notes to work with.

If you started out playing a four-string and have moved on to five, you can use the octave pattern to identify the notes on the fifth string, as shown below.

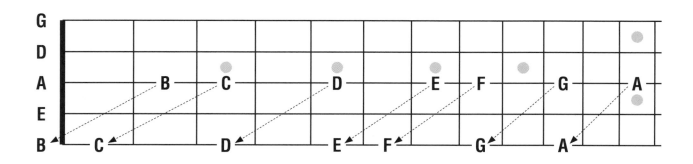

Drop D Tuning

Drop D tuning is pretty common in rock and metal, and you're sure to encounter it if you haven't already. Drop D involves detuning the lowest string (fourth string) by one whole step, from E to D. This gives you an extra low open D to work with and is mainly used to write songs and riffs in D major or D minor. The rest of the strings on the bass remain in standard tuning, giving you the tuning (low to high): D–A–D–G.

In terms of your scale patterns and arpeggios, the detuned string throws them all a little out of whack. You can still play them normally on the upper three strings, but you'll need to make some adjustments if you want to incorporate the low string. That's something you can explore later on your own, once we've covered the material in future chapters. Right now, we'll just help you identify the notes in the new tuning.

The first thing you'll notice is the note names on the fourth string now match the notes on the second string, but one octave lower. If you've got the second-string notes memorized, it will be easier for you to keep track of the detuned fourth string. You should also be aware that all of the pitches that you knew when the string was tuned to E will now be shifted up two frets—the E is now at the second fret, the G is at the fifth fret, the A is at the seventh fret, etc. The more you play in drop D, the more familiar you'll be with the placement of these pitches. Do your best to think ahead a little while you're playing so you don't accidentally hit the wrong notes. The fretboard diagram, notation, and tab below show the natural notes on the fourth string in drop D tuning.

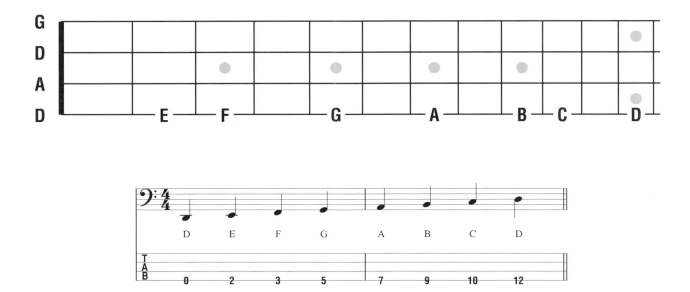

One convenient thing about drop D is that the octave pattern between the second and fourth strings has shifted by two frets. The octave notes are now located at the same fret, making it very easy to incorporate them into your bass lines. The following fretboard diagram demonstrates this at a few select frets.

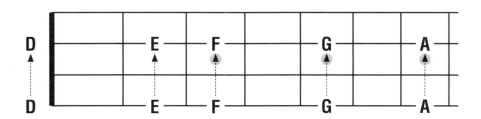

REVIEW QUIZ

Identify the notes in the following fretboard diagrams. Answers are located at the bottom of the page.

1.
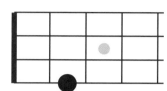

2.
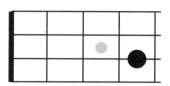

3.
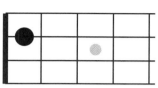

4.
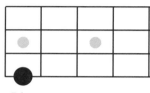

5 fr.

5.
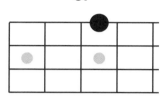

5 fr.

6.
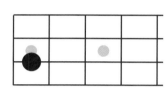

7 fr.

7.
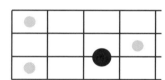

12 fr.

8.
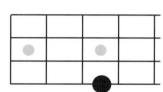

7 fr.

9.
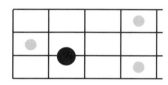

9 fr.

QUICK REVIEW:

- You can use the musical alphabet's half-step and whole-step formula to locate any natural note on the bass.

- For any note on the third or fourth strings, its octave is located two frets and two strings higher.

- The notes at the 12th fret are exactly one octave higher than the open strings.

- The notes at the fifth fret are identical to their next higher open string.

- The notes at the seventh fret are one octave higher than the open strings below them.

Chapter 3: The Major Scale

The *major scale* represents the foundation of most scales and chords in Western music. The notes are famously showcased in the song "Do-Re-Mi" from *The Sound of Music*. Major scales contain seven notes, arranged using consecutive letters of the musical alphabet, with a specific order of whole steps and half steps. This series of intervals is known as an *intervallic formula*, and it's the same for every major scale, no matter what the key is.

THE C MAJOR SCALE

If you count up from C to C in the musical alphabet (C–D–E–F–G–A–B–C), you'll have the C major scale. C major is unique in that it contains all natural notes (no sharps or flats).

Below is one octave of the C major scale, beginning at the third fret on the third string. The tablature and fretboard diagram represent just one suggested finger pattern for the major scale; we'll explore other options for playing the scale shortly. In the diagram, the C notes are indicated with white dots. This note is called the *tonic* (often referred to as the *root note*). The tonic is the first note, or *degree*, of the scale and gives the scale its letter name.

TRACK 18   C Major Scale

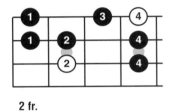

2 fr.

Intervals of the Major Scale

In the previous chapters, we discussed how natural half steps occur in the musical alphabet between the notes B and C, and E and F. With this knowledge, we can examine the C major scale and deduce that the half steps occur between the 3rd and 4th, and 7th and 8th (octave) degrees of the scale. This information gives us the intervallic formula W–W–H–W–W–W–H for the major scale. All major scales, no matter what key, contain this same unique order of half steps and whole steps.

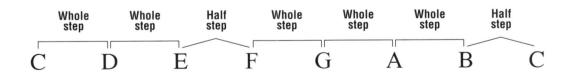

In most rock, blues, and jazz music, the major scale may not be the most go-to scale for bass lines; it has a tendency to sound too sterile, with little flavor or character, unless it's used sparingly against the right chord progression. However, since the major scale represents the basis of all other scales and establishes the fundamental rules of music theory, it's essential for us to examine its formula and get acquainted with it on the bass.

The following examples show how you can use the notes of the C major scale to create simple, melodic bass lines against a chord progression in the key of C major. Both examples contain only the notes in the one-octave scale shown on the previous page.

TRACK 19

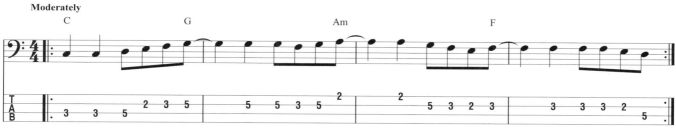

TRACK 20

In music theory, the degrees (or steps) of a scale are usually indicated by numbers, making it easier to study and examine the relationships between intervals, regardless of the key. If we use the C major scale as an example, the note D would be called the 2nd, the note E would be called the 3rd, and so on. The example below shows the C major scale with the intervals indicated above the notation (W = whole step; H = half step), and the numbered steps of the scale indicated between the notation and tab.

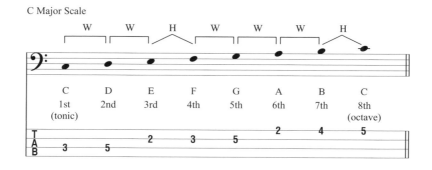

So far, we've only discussed the intervals of half steps and whole steps, which are usually used to refer to the space between adjacent notes. Music theory is the study of many different intervals, and each step of the major scale is a specific distance (interval) from the tonic. By referring to the example on the previous page, we can see that the distance from C to D is called a *2nd*, the distance from C to E is called a *3rd*, the distance from C to F is called a *4th*, and so on. Of course, the note F is the fourth step of the scale, but it is also referred to as "the 4th" in the key of C, with the term "4th" indicating the name of the musical distance from C (the tonic) to F (the fourth note of the scale). Don't worry if it's a little confusing right now; it will get easier the more we use the terminology.

There are also different variations of these intervals—for example, *major 3rds* and *minor 3rds*. For now, let's just look at the specific types of intervals that are unique to the major scale:

- The 1st step is called the *tonic* (or root note).
- The 2nd step is called a *major 2nd*.
- The 3rd step is called a *major 3rd*.
- The 4th step is called a *perfect 4th*.
- The 5th step is called a *perfect 5th*.
- The 6th step is called a *major 6th*.
- The 7th step is called a *major 7th*.
- The 8th step is called the *octave* (also the tonic, or root note).

What Makes an Interval Perfect?

You may be wondering why most of the intervals in the major scale are called *major* (major 2nd, major 3rd, major 6th, and major 7th), while a few are called *perfect* (perfect 4th, perfect 5th). Don't be concerned with it at this point—they're just names. In fact, when musicians are communicating with each other, they usually drop the "perfect" modifier and just called them "4ths" and "5ths" (even though musicians usually use the major and minor terms for the other intervals). This has something to do with the fact that both the 4th and 5th are the same distance from the tonic in both major and minor keys. Regardless, it's not something you need to worry about right now. Later on, we'll talk about other types of 4ths and 5ths, but it will be on a need-to-know basis.

TRANSPOSING THE MAJOR SCALE

The great thing about the tuning of the bass guitar is that all of the scale patterns remain the same, no matter what fret or string you start them on. That means that once you've learned the C major scale, you can transpose it to any key by just starting the exact same pattern at a different fret. This is one of the reasons why it's so essential for you to learn the notes on the fretboard—to make it easy to transpose scales to other keys.

If we move the C major scale two frets up the fretboard (one whole step higher), we'll have a D major scale, shown on the following page in notation and tab, with a scale diagram on the right.

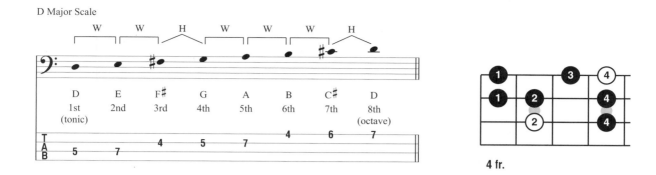

D Major Scale

You'll notice that the key of D major contains two sharps—F♯ and C♯. These are necessary because we have to manipulate the notes in the musical alphabet in order to maintain our major scale formula, W–W–H–W–W–W–H, and make sure we have the correct order of half steps and whole steps when D is the tonic. By raising the letter F to F♯, we now have the correct whole step between the 2nd and 3rd degrees of the scale (which also creates the necessary half step between the 3rd and 4th). Similarly, we needed to raise the 7th degree to C♯ in order to achieve the proper intervals there. By using the two sharps, all of the intervals fall into place, giving us a flawless D major scale.

Now let's transpose the major scale to a key that uses flats. Start the same major scale finger pattern on the fourth string at the sixth fret and you'll have a B♭ major scale.

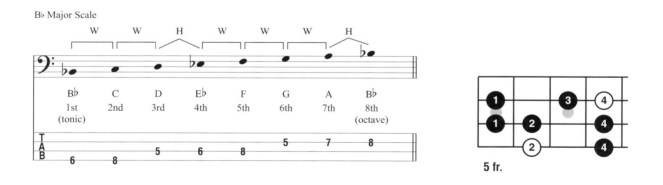

B♭ Major Scale

The key of B♭ major contains two flats—B♭ and E♭. The distance from the tonic, B♭, to the 2nd, C, is already a whole step; we just need to place a flat on the letter E to give us the necessary half step between the 3rd and 4th degrees of the scale (D to E♭) to keep our major scale formula, W–W–H–W–W–W–H, intact. When determining the notes in these scales, remember that the letter names must progress consecutively through the musical alphabet, letter by letter; this is why we use the note E♭, as opposed to D♯.

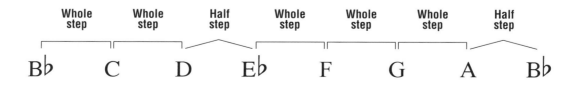

Here are a few coordination exercises you can use to practice the major scale fingering. This first example shows the scale played in groups of three: first ascending, then descending. Start out with the C major scale, beginning at the third fret on the third string. After completing the pattern, move it up one fret to play the pattern a half step higher. Continue to transpose and play the pattern one fret at a time all the way up the fretboard until you reach the C major scale one octave higher (at the 15th fret). The actual *key signatures* have been used in the notation for reading convenience. This is a great warm-up that you can apply to other scales, too.

TRACK 21

Moderately slow

Here's another exercise that ascends and descends the C major scale in 3rds. As with the example above, transpose the pattern one fret at a time chromatically until you reach the octave (at the 15th fret).

TRACK 22

Moderately slow

32

ALTERNATE SCALE FINGERINGS

The major scale fingering we've explored so far is probably the most comfortable for beginners to play, but there are a few other useful fingerings for the one-octave major scale, too. Learning these alternate fingerings will allow you to visualize the scale and its intervals in different ways on the fretboard while still using the same pitches. At the same time, we'll take this opportunity to look at some of the more complicated key signatures that use numerous accidentals.

Let's check out the E major scale beginning at the seventh fret on the third string. The alternate fingering shown here starts with the first finger and contains some wider stretches than previously used. Follow the tab and the scale diagram closely to be sure you're playing the correct notes. The key of E major contains four sharps: F♯, G♯, C♯, and D♯.

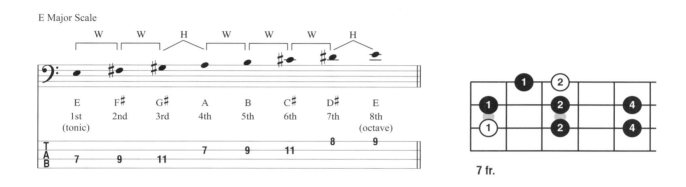

To get the correct pitches for the scale when using the W–W–H–W–W–W–H major scale formula, start with the note E and add sharps where needed to establish the proper intervals. We need a sharp on F to give us a whole step for the 2nd, then another sharp on G to give us the next whole step. From there, the natural notes A and B are OK as is, but we'll need to adds sharps to C and D to complete the formula.

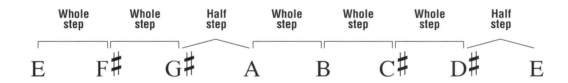

Here's a fun rock riff in E major that uses the scale fingering shown above. Listen to the track to hear the phrasing, then give it a shot. You can also transpose this to other keys by moving the finger pattern to different places on the fretboard.

TRACK 23

Here's the G♭ major scale using the scale fingering from the previous page, this time starting on the fourth string at the second fret. The frets are further apart in this area of the fretboard, making the stretch a bit more difficult.

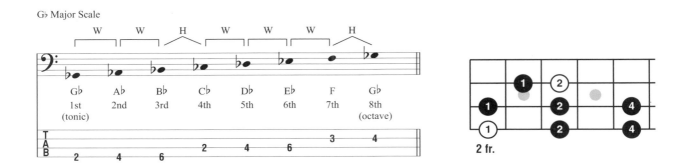

The key of G♭ major is almost entirely made up of flat notes, the only exception being the 7th (F). Also notice that this key contains the note C♭, which we haven't encountered yet. You'll remember that the musical alphabet contains a natural half step between the notes B and C; however, we've already used B♭ for the 3rd, so theoretically, we'll need to use the letter name C for the 4th step while still maintaining our major scale formula. The only way to do this is to lower the C by a half step to make it a C♭—even though the notes B and C♭ are played at the same fret and are the exact same pitch. Any two note names that share the same pitch are said to be enharmonically equivalent. This phenomenon can occur in similar instances where music theory requires it. For example, the notes E♯ and F are also enharmonically equivalent.

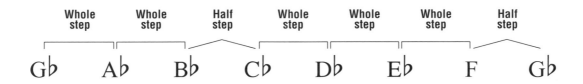

The following coordination exercise utilizes the above major scale fingering played in groups of four—first ascending, then descending. Start at the third fret in G major, then move the pattern chromatically up the fretboard to the octave G at the 15th fret.

TRACK 24

Moderately slow

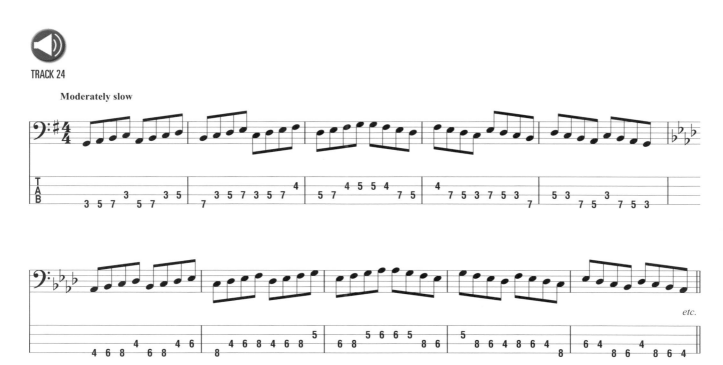

34

Here's our third and final fingering for the one-octave major scale, starting with your fourth finger on the fourth string. Let's put this one in the key of B major, which contains five sharps.

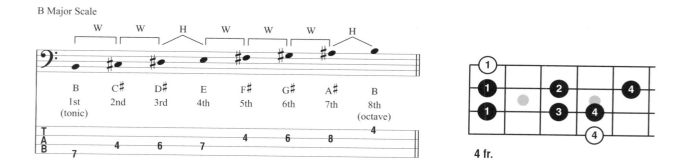

B Major Scale

Starting on B and adhering to the W–W–H–W–W–W–H major scale formula, we'll need to add sharps to almost every note, the sole exception being the 4th (E).

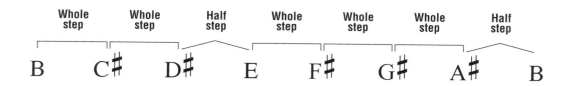

Whole step	Whole step	Half step	Whole step	Whole step	Whole step	Half step
B	C♯	D♯	E	F♯	G♯	A♯	B

MUSIC THEORY APPLICATIONS

In Chapter 2, we explored how you can use the half step, whole step, and octave intervals to help you identify the notes on the fretboard. Once you've memorized the fretboard, you can use the major scale finger patterns to find the note name of a specific interval. For example, if you want to know what the 3rd is in the key of C major, find the tonic C on the fretboard and use the major scale finger pattern to locate the third note in the scale, as shown in the diagram below. By referring to the scale pattern, you can easily identify the 3rd as the note E.

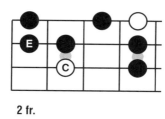

2 fr.

This is an important concept that we'll use in depth later on. Oftentimes, you'll need to identify an interval's note name when creating bass lines, improvising, or working with other musicians in general. Since all of the scale patterns are moveable and easily transposed, you can use the patterns to find the answers to questions such as, "What is the 4th in A major?" Simply find the root note, A (fifth fret, fourth string), visualize the major scale pattern on the fretboard, and locate the fourth note of the scale. You can see from the diagram below that the 4th is the note D (fifth fret, third string).

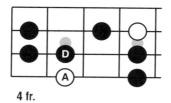

4 fr.

Let's try one more example and locate the 6th in the key of G major. Starting on G at the third fret on string 4, visualize the major scale pattern and count up to the sixth note of the scale. You can see below that the 6th is located at the second fret on string 2: the note E.

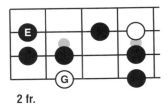

2 fr.

Mastering the Scales

It's essential to learn the scale forms and patterns before you can apply them musically, so for now, concentrate on the scale exercises and memorization. You'll find many ways to use music theory in real-world applications once you have the basic rules down. Take as much time as you need to review and digest the content. If anything seems confusing so far, or you feel lost, go back and review the major scale formula again. Understanding the concept of music theory and its applications involves a steep learning curve. If you're not understanding the theory just yet, memorize the rules for now. At some point, you'll have a breakthrough that will put everything into focus. We're spending a lot of time on the major scale because it represents the foundation of most of the other scales and music theory concepts you'll encounter in the future.

THE FIVE PATTERNS OF THE MAJOR SCALE

Even though there are only seven different note names in the major scale, we can use five comfortable patterns to play it across the entire fretboard. The following five G major scale patterns contain all of the notes that are playable in G major in specific areas of the fretboard. Pay close attention to the indicated fingerings in patterns 2 and 5; you'll notice that the fourth finger can be used to comfortably pivot your hand by one fret, making the full scale position easier to play. These suggested fingerings don't need to be strictly followed, and the fourth-finger pivot is only useful when you are ascending or descending through that particular part of each scale pattern. You can easily alter the fingerings to make them more comfortable, depending on the context.

G Major Scale: Pattern 1

TRACK 25

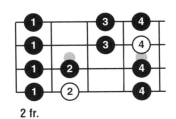

2 fr.

G Major Scale: Pattern 2

TRACK 26

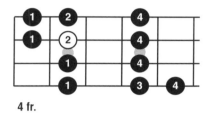

4 fr.

G Major Scale: Pattern 3

TRACK 27

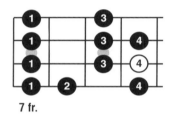

7 fr.

G Major Scale: Pattern 4

TRACK 28

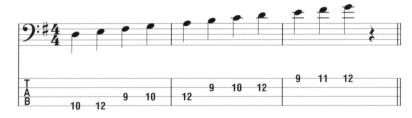

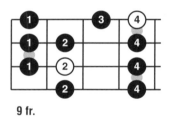

9 fr.

G Major Scale: Pattern 5

TRACK 29

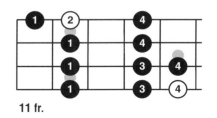

11 fr.

The following exercise shows a good way to practice the five patterns of the G major scale. It should be played continuously in steady eighth notes; the odd time signatures are there for reading convenience so that each pattern is represented within two measures (the patterns are indicated above the notation). Start by ascending the first pattern in 3rds, then pivot up to the second pattern and descend in 3rds. Continue in this fashion up the fretboard through all five patterns, then back down the fretboard until you reach the first pattern again. Some fret-hand fingerings have been included below the notation to clarify the position changes. Once you've got it down, transpose the scale patterns and practice them in other keys.

TRACK 30

Since the major scale represents the foundation for most of the other scales in popular music, the previous five scale fingerings will be seen many times in future chapters. We can transpose them to other keys, or we may change the placement of the root notes to derive other scales from them, but the finger patterns themselves will mostly remain the same. This is why it's essential for you to memorize them now. It may seem like a lot of material right out of the gate, but if you get these patterns down cold, the content coming up in future chapters will be much easier.

TWO-OCTAVE MAJOR SCALE

The purpose of learning and practicing two-octave scales is to help you to break the mindset of being locked into one position and to visualize a scale across the entire fretboard. Just playing a scale in one place from root note to octave and back down is a good way to start, but it's not as useful in practical applications. The following two-octave major scale can be added to your practice and warm-up routines to help you gain speed and accuracy in moving around the neck. When you're improvising, you'll probably just play sections of these scales and do something more creative and musical with them. The scale diagrams and fingerings shown here are suggestions to get you started, but you might discover different fingerings that are more comfortable for you personally, so experiment and alter them if you wish.

Let's start out with a two-octave C major scale. The notation and tab below show the scale ascending and descending, with the left-hand fingerings indicated underneath the notation staff. The two scale diagrams below the music also show the suggested fingerings, with arrows indicating where you can slide up (or down) to switch positions. Slide lines have been included in the notation and tab to show where the position shifts occur. You'll notice that we've suggested sliding up with the third finger while ascending, and down with the first finger while descending. As with other scale fingerings, this is just a suggestion; feel free to try alternatives.

TRACK 31

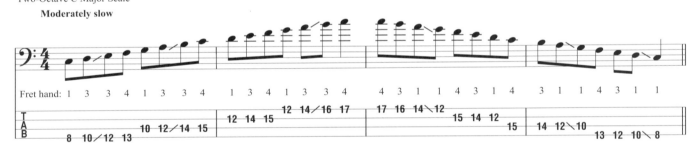

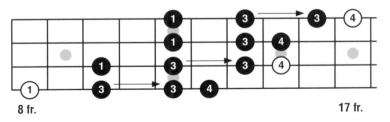

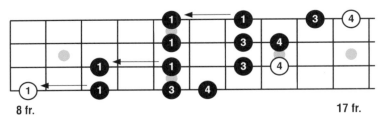

Now let's transpose the two-octave scale to some other popular keys. The first is G major, and it follows the same finger pattern as the C major scale on the previous page, this time starting on the third fret.

TRACK 32

Two-Octave G Major Scale
Moderately slow

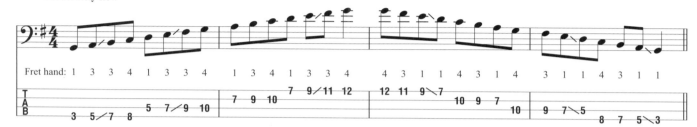

Here's a bass riff played in G major using most of the notes of the two-octave scale. Use the fingering shown above.

TRACK 33

Moderately slow

Playing the two-octave E major scale is a bit easier since it starts in open position; you can cover two full octaves without using as many position shifts.

TRACK 34

Two-Octave E Major Scale
Moderately slow

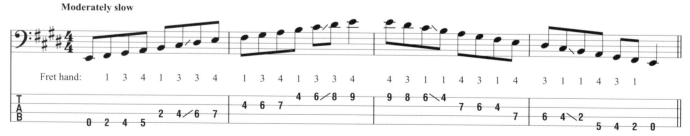

The following bass line uses parts of the two-octave scale to weave its way through a chord change in the key of E major.

TRACK 35

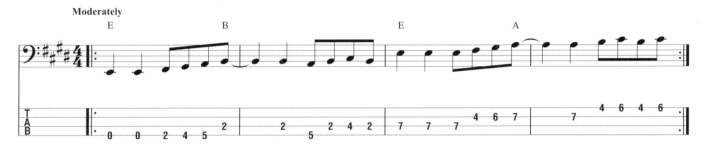

REVIEW QUIZ

Use the half-step/whole-step formula for the major scale (W–W–H–W–W–W–H) to add the necessary accidentals to the following major keys. Answers are at the bottom of the following page.

1. F Major Scale

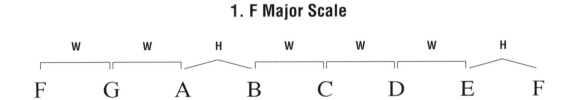

2. A Major Scale

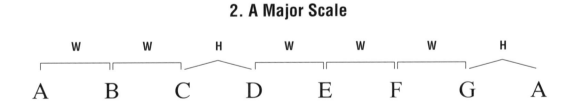

3. E♭ Major Scale

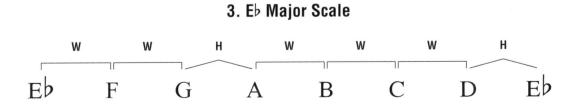

Use the one-octave major scale finger patterns to identify the note names of each of the following intervals. Answers are at the bottom of the page.

4. The 3rd of G

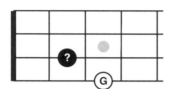

5. The 5th of F

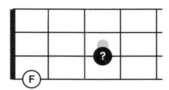

6. The 4th of A

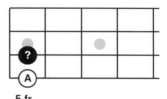

5 fr.

7. The 5th of D

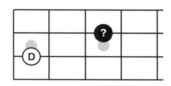

5 fr.

8. The 6th of C

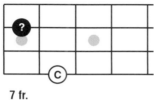

7 fr.

9. The 6th of E

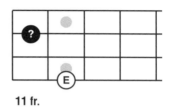

11 fr.

QUICK REVIEW:

- The intervallic formula for the major scale is W–W–H–W–W–W–H.

- You can transpose the major scale to another key by beginning the major scale finger pattern at a different fret.

- You can use the major scale finger patterns and your knowledge of the fretboard to find the note names of specific intervals in the scale.

- You can comfortably play the notes in the major scale anywhere on the fretboard by using five different scale patterns.

Answer Key

1. F–G–A–Bb–C–D–E–F

2. A–B–C#–D–E–F#–G#–A

3. Eb–F–G–Ab–Bb–C–D–Eb

4. B

5. C

6. D

7. A

8. A

9. C#

Chapter 4: The Minor Scale

Another essential scale used in all styles of music is the minor scale. Compared to the major scale, the minor scale has a dark, or melancholy, characteristic. Western music has incorporated a few altered versions of the minor scale that we'll look at later on, but for this lesson, we'll focus on the original and most popular version: the *natural minor scale* (also referred to as simply the *minor scale*).

THE A MINOR SCALE

The A minor scale contains only natural notes (no sharps or flats). By playing through the notes of the musical alphabet from A to the next higher A, you'll have the A minor scale. Below is one octave of the A minor scale, beginning at the fifth fret of the fourth string. The scale is shown in notation and tab, with a scale diagram on the right.

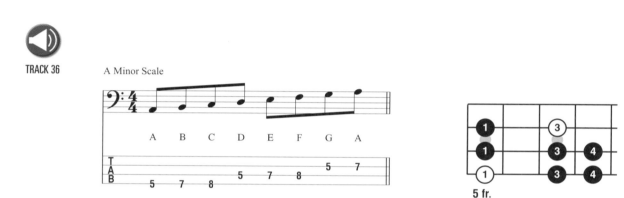

Intervals of the Minor Scale

The natural minor scale yields its own unique order of half steps and whole steps (W–H–W–W–H–W–W), as shown below. The natural half steps in the minor scale occur between the 2nd and 3rd, and 5th and 6th degrees of the scale. All of the other intervals in the scale are whole steps. All natural minor scales, no matter what key, contain this same series of half steps and whole steps.

The basic tonal characteristic of the minor scale comes from the lowered (flatted) 3rd. In minor keys, the 3rd is one-and-a-half steps above the tonic (root note), whereas in major keys, the 3rd is two whole steps above the tonic. The ♭3rd is what gives the minor scale its dark and sad tonality. The ♭6th and ♭7th also distinguish it from the major scale and contribute to the minor scale's tonal quality.

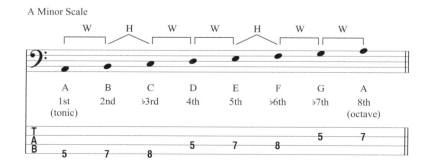

43

Here's a list of the specific intervals in the natural minor scale:

- The 1st step is the *tonic* (or root).
- The 2nd step is a *major 2nd*.
- The 3rd step is a *minor 3rd*.
- The 4th step is a *perfect 4th*.
- The 5th step is a *perfect 5th*.
- The 6th step is a *minor 6th*.
- The 7th step is a *minor 7th*.
- The 8th step is the *octave* (or tonic/root).

Different Types of Intervals

All intervals have two distinct characteristics: *quantity* and *quality*. The quantity is the numeric value between letter-name notes in the alphabet. For example, A and B are a 2nd apart, A and C are a 3rd apart, and so on. The quality distinguishes the interval further by adding a descriptive term such as "major" or "minor." The interval from A and B is called a *major 2nd* since it is the distance of one whole step. The interval from B to C is called a *minor 2nd* since it is the distance of one half step. Similarly, you'll notice that a minor 3rd is one half step lower than a major 3rd, and a minor 6th is one half step lower than a major 6th. We'll explore other interval qualities later on, such as *augmented* and *diminished*, which are used to alter the perfect 4ths and 5ths.

The following example is a rock/metal-style bass line using only the notes from the one-octave A minor scale from the previous page.

TRACK 37

44

TRANSPOSING THE MINOR SCALE

You can easily transpose the closed-position A minor scale to another key by simply starting the scale pattern at a different fret, but where's the fun in that? Let's transpose by using scale theory instead so that we can determine where the accidentals are and at the same time come up with some alternative fingerings for the scale.

First, let's take a look at the B minor scale. In order to achieve a whole step between the 1st and 2nd steps of the scale, we need to add a sharp to the note C, which in turn will give us the necessary half step between the 2nd and 3rd steps (C♯ to D). Using the same principle, we will add a sharp to the note F to give us the necessary whole step between the 4th and 5th, along with the necessary half step between the 5th and 6th. All of the other intervals fit with the scale formula; therefore, the key of B minor contains two sharps—C♯ and F♯.

Below is the B minor scale shown in notation and tab, with a scale diagram on the right. We've used a different fingering this time that starts with your second finger at the seventh fret on the fourth string. This one involves some fairly wide finger stretches, so you'll probably find it more useful and comfortable to play the pattern further up the fretboard where the frets are closer together.

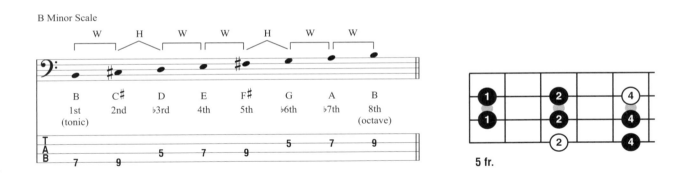

The following example is a B minor riff using the above scale fingering. Oftentimes, the context of a bass line or riff will be instrumental in determining which scale pattern works best. In this case, the series of hammer-ons and pull-offs are easily accomplished by using this particular scale fingering.

TRACK 38

Now let's transpose the minor scale to a key that uses flats: C minor. In order to achieve the minor 3rd, we'll first need to flat the E, giving us the necessary half step between the 2nd and 3rd steps of the scale. The next two whole-step intervals are OK as is, but we need to flat the A in order to get the correct minor 6th of the scale. The B also needs a flat to give us the proper whole step between the 6th and 7th steps. The notes of the C minor scale are shown below with the three flatted notes in the key: Eb, Ab, and Bb.

Here's the C minor scale shown in notation and tab, along with a scale diagram. Let's use another new fingering for this one, starting with the fourth finger at the eighth fret on the fourth string.

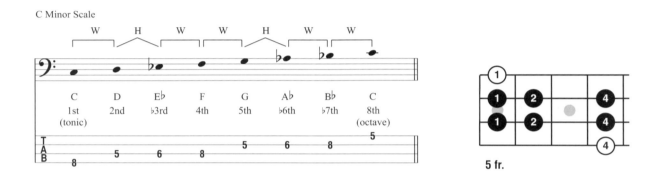

This next example is a bass line in C minor using the above scale fingering. The line includes hammer-ons and pull-offs to demonstrate how this particular scale fingering is preferable here.

TRACK 39

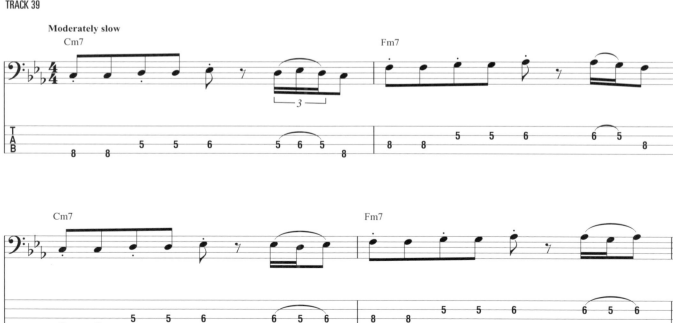

RELATIVE MAJOR AND MINOR SCALES

Relative scales are scales that share all of the same notes, but start and end on different tonics. For example, since the A minor scale contains only natural notes, it is the *relative minor* of C major. Conversely, the C major scale is the *relative major* of A minor. Every major scale has a relative minor scale that starts on its 6th step, as shown in the following diagram that compares the C major and A minor scales.

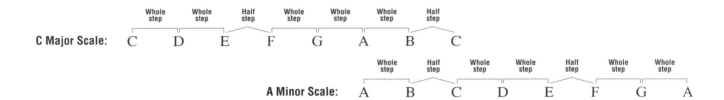

You can determine any major scale's relative minor on the fretboard by using the major scale finger pattern. Simply visualize or play the major scale until you reach the 6th note, which will tell you the name of its relative minor key. Here's an example using the C major scale fretboard diagram.

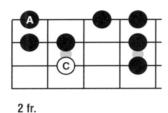

2 fr.

Let's reverse the process and start with the minor scale. Every minor scale has a relative major scale that starts on its 3rd step, as shown in the chart below with the A minor and C major scales.

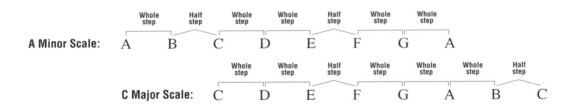

The relative major scale can be found by playing the minor scale finger pattern on the bass until you reach the 3rd note in the scale, shown below using the A minor scale starting at the fifth fret on the fourth string.

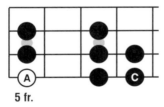

5 fr.

If you reverse the process, you'll notice that you can also locate the major scale's relative minor by counting backwards from the root—in this case, counting backwards from the note C at the eighth fret to its relative minor at the fifth fret, A.

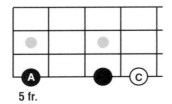

5 fr.

In either case, the quickest shortcut to finding a relative major or minor scale is to visualize that their tonic notes are always a minor 3rd (three frets) apart. Any major scale's relative minor starts a minor 3rd *below* its tonic, and any minor scale's relative major starts a minor 3rd *above* its tonic.

All of this information can be helpful in figuring out how many sharps or flats are in any given key. For example, if you want to determine what the notes are in B minor, you can locate its relative major scale a minor 3rd higher, D major. If you already know that the key of D major contains two sharps (F♯ and C♯), then it follows that the key of B minor will also contain those same notes.

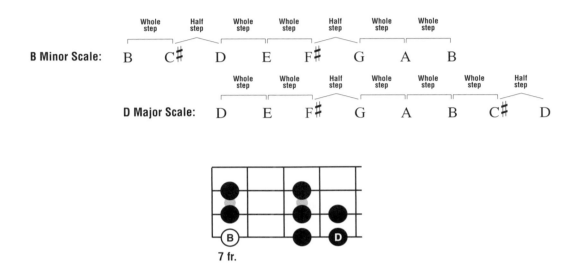

You can determine if a song or section of a song is in a major or minor key by figuring out what the tonic is. If the music has no sharps or flats, but begins and ends on an A minor chord, it's a pretty safe bet that the song is in the key of A minor. The tonic will sound like "home"—where the music resolves to. Relative major and minor keys are often used together in the same piece of music. It's common for a song to have a verse and chorus in a major key, then *modulate* (change keys) to its relative minor for the bridge in order to give it a fresh tonal landscape. Here's an example that uses C major for the first section, then modulates to the relative A minor for the second section.

TRACK 40

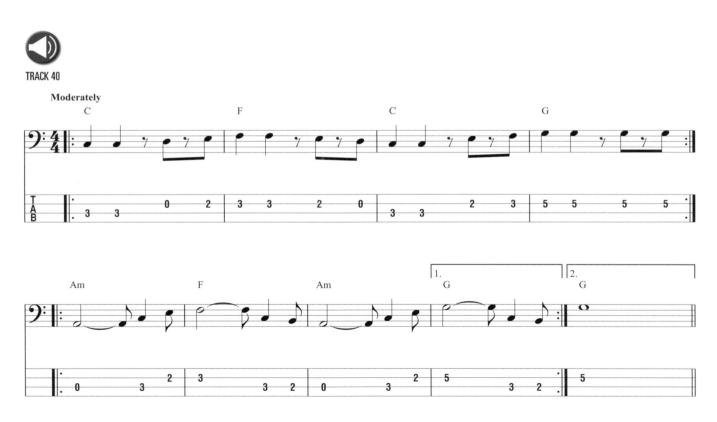

THE FIVE PATTERNS OF THE MINOR SCALE

Here are the five E minor scale patterns that can be used to span the entire fretboard. Since you already learned the G major patterns in the last chapter, and E minor is the relative minor of G major, you don't need to relearn the patterns—they are identical; however, the placement of the root notes is different. In order to use these successfully in minor keys, you'll need to memorize where all of the root notes are located within the patterns. We've also renumbered the order of the scale patterns to reflect the minor key, starting with the first pattern on the tonic E at the 12th fret on the fourth string.

E Minor Scale: Pattern 1

TRACK 41

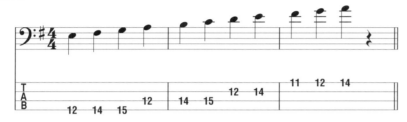

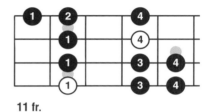

11 fr.

E Minor Scale: Pattern 2

TRACK 42

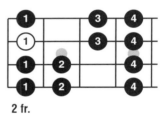

2 fr.

E Minor Scale: Pattern 3

TRACK 43

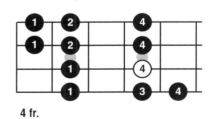

4 fr.

E Minor Scale: Pattern 4

TRACK 44

 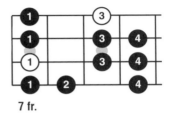

E Minor Scale: Pattern 5

TRACK 45

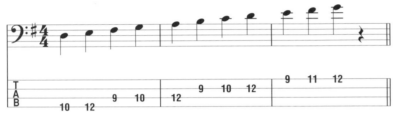 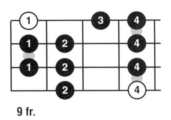

Since the key of E minor is easily played in open position, let's take this opportunity to transpose the first pattern down an octave.

E Minor Scale: Pattern 1 (Open)

TRACK 46

 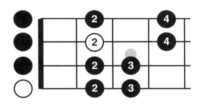

Here's a new scale exercise, shown at the top of the next page, using the first two scale patterns. Start out by ascending pattern 1 in open position, then move up and descend pattern 2. Continue in this fashion all the way up the fretboard, then reverse direction and work your way back down the fretboard. You can use the scale exercises from the previous chapter to practice the E minor scale patterns.

Moderately slow

Pattern 1

Pattern 2

etc.

Transposing the Scale Patterns

These scale patterns are easily transposed by moving them all an equal number of frets in any direction, but the real secret to applying them is to visualize and memorize where the root notes are located in each pattern. The root notes should stand out like a beacon in your mind's eye so that, wherever they fall on the neck, no matter what the key is, you'll be able to visualize the appropriate scale pattern around those notes. You've already seen that the patterns themselves are identical for relative keys, except for the placement of the root notes, so the only way to distinguish major from minor is in how you apply the scale patterns musically. The root notes should be considered home and should function in that way. This is a concept we'll revisit many times, especially in the future chapter on modes. Let's transpose the patterns to the key of D minor (shown below). We'll apply them to a bass solo in the key of D minor on the following page.

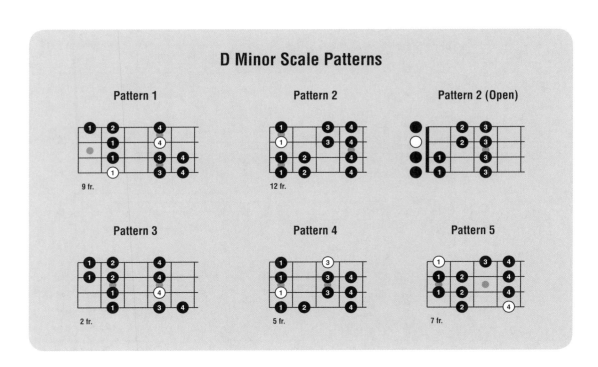

D Minor Scale Patterns

Pattern 1   Pattern 2   Pattern 2 (Open)

9 fr.   12 fr.

Pattern 3   Pattern 4   Pattern 5

2 fr.   5 fr.   7 fr.

Here's a short solo in D minor that utilizes notes from the different patterns shown on the previous page. The fret-hand fingering is included above the tab to indicate where the position shifts occur. Remember to keep track of your root notes so you'll always have a solid tonal center to come back to when playing riffs and melodies.

TRACK 48

Moderately
Half-time feel

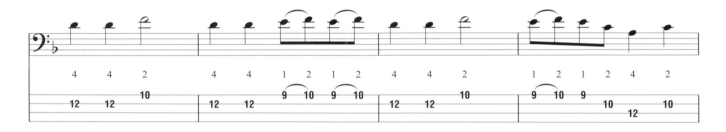

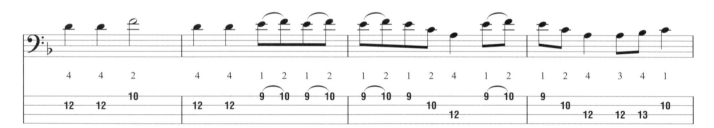

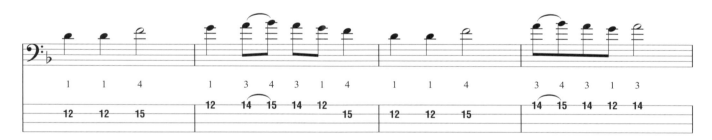

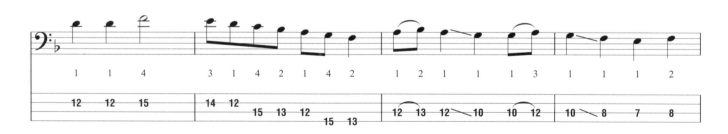

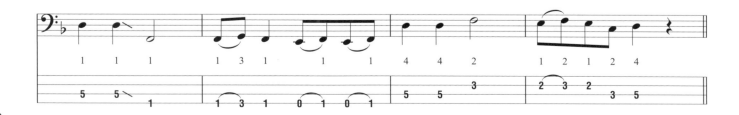

TWO-OCTAVE MINOR SCALE

The following two-octave A minor scale starts on the fourth string at the fifth fret. The minor scale is a little more difficult to map out as a two-octave pattern because of the order of the intervals. In the ascending version, we are using the fourth finger to slide up and shift positions. In the descending version, most of the downward slides are executed with the first finger, with the exception of the slide on the first string. Here, we've chosen to slide downward with the fourth finger so we can avoid an otherwise uncomfortable stretch.

TRACK 49

Two-Octave A Minor Scale

Moderately slow

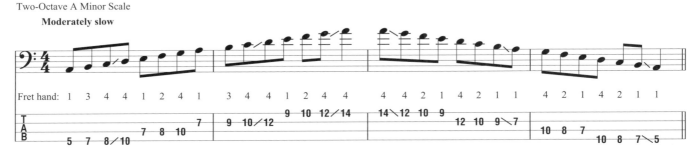

Two-Octave A Minor Scale: Ascending

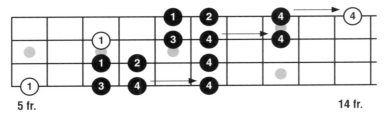

5 fr.   14 fr.

Two-Octave A Minor Scale: Descending

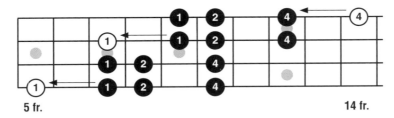

5 fr.   14 fr.

Let's transpose the two-octave minor scale to some other keys. First up is B minor; all you need to do is move the previous pattern up two frets and you've got it.

TRACK 50

Two-Octave B Minor Scale

Moderately slow

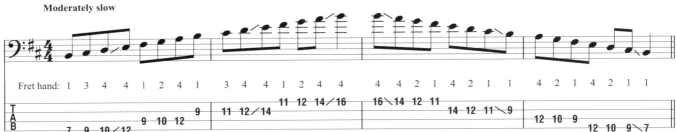

Lastly, let's utilize the low open E string for a two-octave E minor scale. As with the two-octave E major scale in the previous chapter, this one is easier to play since it requires fewer slides and position shifts.

TRACK 51

Two-Octave E Minor Scale

Moderately slow

REVIEW QUIZ

Use the half-step/whole-step formula for the minor scale (W–H–W–W–H–W–W) to add the necessary accidentals to the following minor keys. Answers are at the bottom of the following page.

1. D Minor Scale

2. F# Minor Scale

3. F Minor Scale

4. B♭ Minor Scale

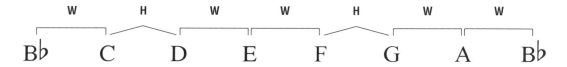

5. What is the relative minor of D major?

6. What is the relative minor of G major?

7. What is the relative minor of B♭ major?

8. What is the relative minor of A♭ major?

9. What is the relative major of F♯ minor?

10. What is the relative major of B♭ minor?

11. What is the relative major of C minor?

12. What is the relative major of D♯ minor?

QUICK REVIEW:

- The intervallic formula for the minor scale is W–H–W–W–H–W–W.
- The minor 3rd is what gives the minor scale its dark and sad tonality.
- Relative scales are scales that share all of the same notes but start and end on different tonics.
- Every major scale has a relative minor scale that starts on its 6th step.
- Every minor scale has a relative major scale that starts on its 3rd step.
- It's common to modulate to a relative major or minor key for a section of a song in order to establish a fresh tonal landscape.

Answer Key

12. F♯ major
11. E♭ major
10. D♭ major
9. A major

8. F minor
7. G minor
6. E minor
5. B minor

4. B♭–C–D♭–E♭–F–G♭–A♭–B♭
3. F–G–A♭–B♭–C–D♭–E♭–F
2. F♯–G♯–A–B–C♯–D–E–F♯
1. D–E–F–G–A–B♭–C–D

55

Chapter 5: Key Signatures

In written music, *key signatures* are used at the beginning of each line of music to tell us which sharps or flats to apply to the notes throughout. The key signature helps to determine what key the music is in and keeps us from having to clutter up the written music with numerous sharps or flats. Since there are 12 different notes in the musical alphabet (chromatically), there are 12 different key signatures. We have already discussed the major and minor scale formulas, how to determine how many sharps and flats are in the scales, and what notes to apply them to. We also know that the keys of C major and A minor have no sharps or flats, so there will be no sharps or flats next to the clef for those keys. Let's take a look at the other keys and explore a few ways to determine and then memorize the key signatures.

SHARP KEYS

Below are the major key signatures that contain sharps, starting with the key of G major, which has one sharp. The tonic, G, is the 5th step in the key of C major (C–D–E–F–G). The next key, D major, contains two sharps and its tonic, D, is the 5th step of the previous key, G major (G–A–B–C–D). This pattern is no coincidence; it follows for the rest of the keys as well. The note A is the 5th step in the key of D major, so the next key (three sharps) is A major. As you progress through the order of keys, each new key signature contains the same accidentals from the previous key, plus one more. This progression of keys in 5ths continues until we reach the key of F# major (six sharps), the last key to use all sharps.

Each key signature has a relative minor key, which starts on the 6th step of its relative major. Since they share the same key signature, determining if a song is in the major or minor key depends on the musical context. For the most part, if a song starts and ends on a major chord, and the major chords *sounds like* home—where the music resolves—then it's a safe bet that it's in a major key. If it sounds like the music resolves to a minor tonic, then the song is likely in the relative minor key. Below are the relative minor key signatures that use all sharps. Notice that the order of these keys also progresses in 5ths.

FLAT KEYS

Now let's look at the key signatures containing flats, beginning with F major (one flat). The next key signature in order is B♭ (two flats), which is a 4th above F. The key signature after that is E♭ (three flats), which is a 4th above B♭. The order of flat keys continues to progress in 4ths until we reach the key of G♭ major (six flats), the last key to use all flats.

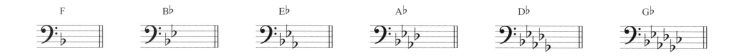

To be thorough, here are the relative minor keys containing all flats, beginning with D minor—the relative minor of F major.

THE CIRCLE OF 5THS

A few observations can be made with respect to the order of key signatures. Notice that the keys F♯ major (six sharps) and G♭ major (six flats) are enharmonically the same—either one can be used since the notes are the same pitches. Also, if you progress through the flat keys in reverse order, each key begins on the 5th of the previous key (the 5th of G♭ [six flats] is D♭ [five flats]; the 5th of D♭ [five flats] is A♭ [four flats], and so on). Using this information, we can lay out the order of the keys in a circle that progresses clockwise in 5ths, known as the *Circle of 5ths*. At the bottom of the circle, the diagram switches from sharps to flats and continues to subtract one flat, key by key, until we arrive at C major again.

You can also navigate the circle counter-clockwise, going through the flat keys first, and the keys will all be a 4th apart. Notice that, when you go through the sharp keys in reverse order, the keys progress in 4ths now, subtracting a sharp for each key until you reach C major at the top.

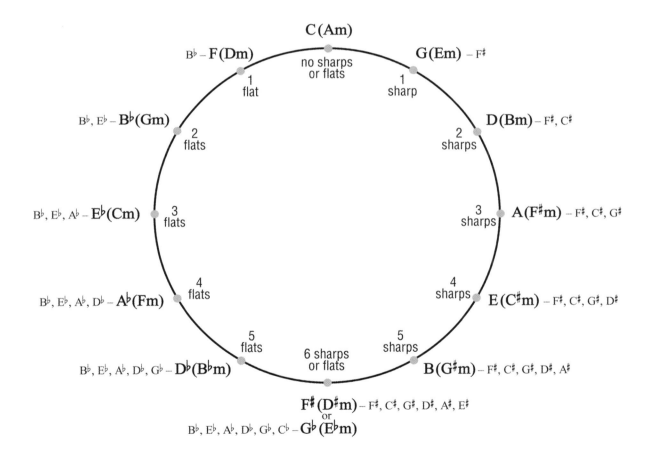

Get familiar with the Circle of 5ths diagram. It can be used to quickly determine how many accidentals are in each key. A good method to help you memorize the order of the keys is to use the circle as a guide while practicing your scales or arpeggios. Begin with the C major scale, then play G major, then D major, and so on, until you make your way through all 12 keys.

Chapter 6: Arpeggios

An *arpeggio* is defined as the notes of a chord played separately. For example, a C major chord is made up of three notes: C, E, and G. If you play those three notes individually on the bass, you're playing a C major arpeggio. Three-note arpeggios are often referred to as *triads*. Knowing your arpeggios and being adept at playing them is invaluable to the bass player because they represent the notes of the chords being played by the rest of the band and will be among the best note choices when constructing your bass lines.

THE MAJOR ARPEGGIO

Let's start out with a simple C major arpeggio fingering. Notice that the notes are the 1st, 3rd, and 5th notes of the C major scale, referred to in musical terms as the tonic, major 3rd, and perfect 5th. The most comfortable way to play the major arpeggio is to start with your second finger on the tonic, as shown below.

C Major Arpeggio

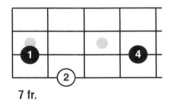

7 fr.

The following exercise begins with major arpeggios at the eighth fret; use the fingering shown in the above diagram. In the second half of the example, move the arpeggio pattern down to the third fret to practice a wider finger stretch.

TRACK 52

Here's an exercise that adds the octave to the major arpeggios.

TRACK 53

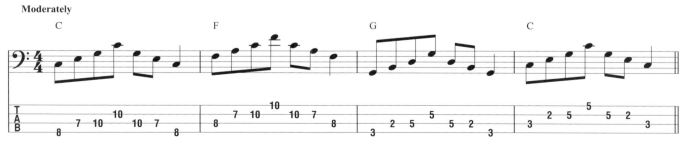

58

Here's an example of a simple bass line in the key of A major using only major arpeggios.

TRACK 54

It isn't necessary to use all of the notes of the arpeggios in succession, as shown above. Remember that these notes are all present in the chords being played, so they represent go-to notes that will fit into your bass lines. The most popular note choice for bass players (outside of the root note and the octave) is the 5th. This next bass line uses only roots, 5ths, and octaves.

TRACK 55

Here's a basic McCartney-esque bass line in the key of A major that demonstrates the strict use of major arpeggios on each chord. In the seventh measure, the 3rd and 5th of the D major arpeggio are played an octave lower, below the root note.

TRACK 56

THE MINOR ARPEGGIO

Now let's take a look at the A minor arpeggio, which consists of the notes A, C, and E—the 1st, 3rd, and 5th notes of the A minor scale. The most comfortable way to play the minor arpeggio is to start out with your first finger on the root note.

A Minor Arpeggio

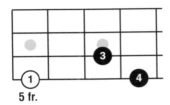

The distance between the root note and the 5th is the same for both the major and minor arpeggios; what differentiates them is the 3rd. In a major arpeggio, the distance from the root note to the 3rd is two whole steps, or a *major 3rd*; in a minor arpeggio, the distance is one-and-a-half steps, or a *minor 3rd*.

Here's an example that uses the minor arpeggio in a bass line in the key of A minor.

TRACK 57

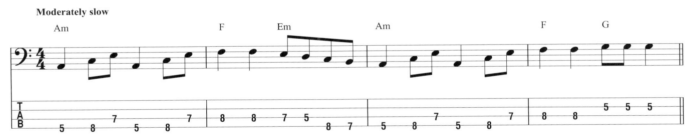

Remember: it's not necessary to use all of the notes of the arpeggio in order. The example below, in D minor, effectively features the minor 3rd to establish a simple melodic theme.

TRACK 58

ALTERNATE ARPEGGIO FINGERINGS

As with the major and minor scales, it's a good idea to learn some other ways to play the arpeggios, in addition to the basic fingerings we've covered so far. Here are some alternate fingerings for the major and minor arpeggios; both require significant five-fret stretches. The major arpeggio starts with your first finger on the root note; the minor arpeggio starts with your second finger on the root note. For practical purposes, we've added the octave to both arpeggios.

C Major Arpeggio

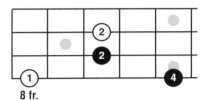

8 fr.

A Minor Arpeggio

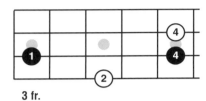

3 fr.

Here are a few more fingerings for the major and minor arpeggios, both starting with your fourth finger on the root notes. You can clearly see the difference between major and minor within these two finger patterns. They're identical, with the sole exception of the 3rd, which is one half step (one fret) lower in the minor arpeggio.

C Major Arpeggio

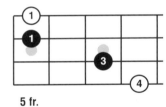

5 fr.

A Minor Arpeggio

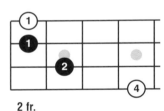

2 fr.

The following exercise reinforces the above concept by incorporating the C major and the C minor arpeggios, both starting with your fourth finger on the root note.

TRACK 59

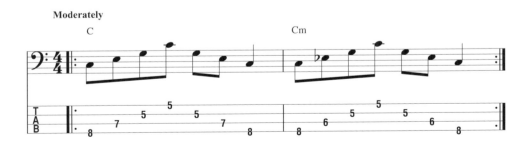

Here's an example that compares the first-finger C major and C minor arpeggios. The suggested fingering is indicated between the notation and tab staves.

TRACK 60

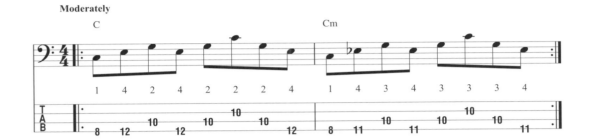

Lastly, here's an example that compares the arpeggios that start with the second finger.

TRACK 61

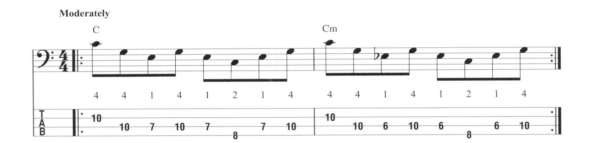

USING THE MAJOR AND MINOR ARPEGGIOS

Here are some bass lines that combine the major and minor arpeggios. This first example is in the key of E minor, using just the E minor and D major arpeggios. We've switched up the order of the notes a bit, rather than simply playing them in R–3–5 order. Sometimes the 3rd or the 5th will be played lower than the root note, making the line sound less generic.

TRACK 62

There are some interesting things about this bass line in D major that we can point out. Notice that the 5th of the D major arpeggio in the first measure is the note A, which is also the root note of the next chord in the progression, A major. This same phenomenon occurs with the A major arpeggio in the second measure; the 5th of the arpeggio is the note E, which is also the root note of the following chord, Em. These are good examples of how to use the notes in the arpeggios to create seamless bass lines that connect the chords in the progression. In addition, the minor 3rd of the E minor arpeggio in the third measure is the note G, the root note of the following chord, G major.

TRACK 63

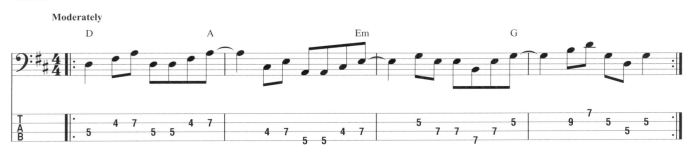

TWO-OCTAVE ARPEGGIOS

By combining some of the previous fingerings, it's possible to play arpeggios seamlessly across two octaves within one position on the fretboard. Remember: it's not necessary to incorporate all of the notes in succession when using these in real-time musical applications, but it's helpful to know that all of these notes are at your disposal.

First up, here's a two-octave G major arpeggio starting with your first finger at the third fret on the fourth string. The example below the diagram is a handy exercise to practice the pattern in triplet groupings.

Two-Octave G Major Arpeggio

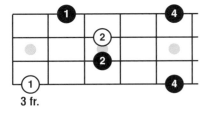

TRACK 64

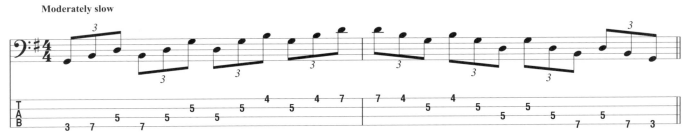

Here's a two-octave B minor arpeggio starting with your first finger at the seventh fret on the fourth string, followed by the triplet pattern exercise in B minor.

Two-Octave B Minor Arpeggio

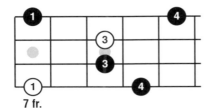

7 fr.

TRACK 65

Moderately slow

Choosing Which Fingerings to Use

Most of the time, arpeggio fingerings are a matter of personal preference. It's natural to shy away from the patterns that use five-fret stretches, or that use the fourth finger for multiple notes at the same fret. It's entirely up to you, but as you progress, you'll find that certain fingerings work better in certain situations, so it's beneficial to memorize and get comfortable with all of the variations. That way, no matter what finger you land on a root note with, you'll always be able to reach for the notes in its arpeggio without shifting positions first.

QUICK REVIEW:

- An arpeggio is defined as the notes of a chord played separately.
- Three-note arpeggios are called triads.
- The notes in a major arpeggio are the tonic, major 3rd, and perfect 5th.
- The notes in a minor arpeggio are the tonic, minor 3rd, and perfect 5th.
- There are three common fingerings for the major and minor arpeggios, each beginning with the first, second, or fourth finger.

Chapter 7: Intervals

In previous chapters, we explored the basic intervals in the musical alphabet and in the major and minor scales. In this chapter, we'll take a more thorough look at the many different intervals and interval patterns in music and how to recognize them on the fretboard. The study of intervals is based upon simple math. For musicians who aren't mathematically inclined, this can be intimidating at first; however, the math here only involves units of measurement and basic addition or subtraction. We'll start this section with a review of the basic concept of intervals and try to break it down into its simplest form to make it easy to understand.

MAJOR AND MINOR 2NDS

As we discussed earlier in this book, an interval describes the distance in pitch between two musical notes. The smallest units of measurement for intervals on the bass are *half steps* (the distance of one fret in either direction on the same string) and *whole steps* (the distance of two frets in either direction on the same string). Half steps and whole steps are the main building blocks of the musical alphabet. The smallest numerical interval in the musical scale is a 2nd, which can refer to either the actual 2nd step of the scale or the distance from one note to the next (or previous note) in the alphabet. A *major 2nd* is the distance of one whole step (or two frets); a *minor 2nd* is the distance of one half step (or one fret). For larger intervals (3rds, 4ths, 5ths, 6ths, etc.), a specific series of whole steps and half steps can be added together in order to arrive at the necessary distance between the two notes.

For simplicity's sake, let's take a look at our trusty C major scale again since it contains only natural notes; therefore, it contains all of the natural half steps and whole steps in the musical alphabet.

When referring to the actual second step of the major scale, we call it *the* major 2nd, because it is a specific scale tone in relationship to the tonic. In the key of C major, the note D is the major 2nd.

We can also use this unit of measurement to describe the distance between two consecutive notes, regardless of the scale or key. For example, since the distance between the notes D and E is a whole step (no matter what key you're in), it can also be said that the interval from D to E is *a major 2nd*. Furthermore, it can be said that the note E is *a major 2nd higher* than the note D, or that the note D is *a major 2nd lower* than the note E.

Notice that in the musical alphabet, the distance between the notes E and F is only a half step. Therefore, it can be said that the interval from E to F is *a minor 2nd*. Furthermore, it can be said that the note F is *a minor 2nd higher* than the note E, or that the note E is *a minor 2nd lower* than the note F.

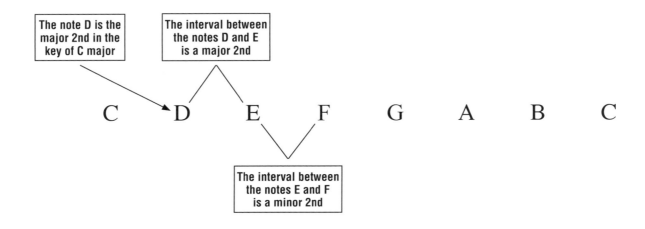

MAJOR AND MINOR 3RDS

In the previous chapter on arpeggios, we discussed major and minor 3rds, so you should already know that the 3rd note in a major scale is called the major 3rd. Taking a look at the C major scale again, we see that the distance from C (the tonic) to E (the major 3rd) is two whole steps; therefore, it follows that any major 3rd interval is also the distance of two whole steps. For example, the interval between the notes F and A is a major 3rd.

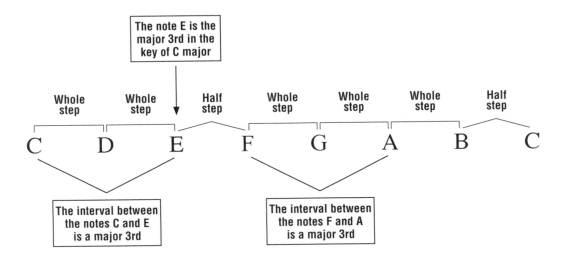

Similar to what we saw with the 2nds, the interval of a minor 3rd is one half step lower than a major 3rd. We already know that the 3rd in the key of A minor (the note C) is a minor 3rd, so let's take a look at our A minor scale again. As you can see in the chart below, the distance from A (the tonic) to C (the minor 3rd) is one-and-a-half steps; therefore, it follows that any minor 3rd interval is also the distance of one-and-a-half steps. For example, the interval between the notes D and F is a minor 3rd.

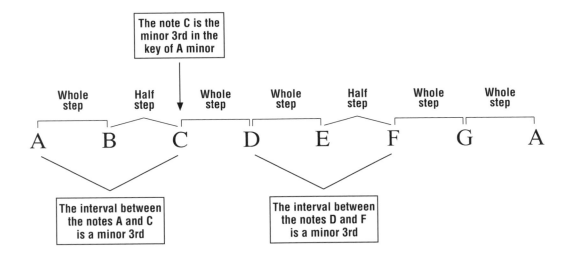

Two commonly used finger patterns for playing a major 3rd and a minor 3rd are shown in the diagrams below. For simplicity, we've used C as the tonic for the major 3rd diagram, and A as the tonic for the minor 3rd diagram, but these patterns are, of course, movable to any other keys on the fretboard. You should recognize both of these interval patterns from the previous chapter on arpeggios. The root notes are white circles; the 3rds are black circles.

Major 3rd

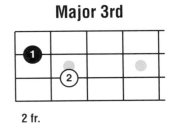

2 fr.

Minor 3rd

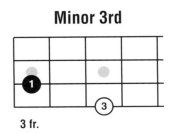

3 fr.

The following exercise incorporates all of the major and minor 3rd intervals that occur naturally in the key of C major. The example begins on the tonic at the third fret on the third string and progresses up the fretboard until reaching the octave, then back down. Use the fingerings shown in the diagrams on the previous page. The purpose of this exercise is twofold: it reinforces the interval patterns for major and minor 3rds, and it will introduce you to where the major and minor 3rd intervals occur in major keys—a concept that will be important in future chapters.

This next exercise is similar to the previous one, but it's played in the key of A minor. We've applied a triplet pattern for the rhythm, but the example still progresses upward through the scale until reaching the octave, then back down. Use the same fingerings for the major and minor 3rds as the previous exercise.

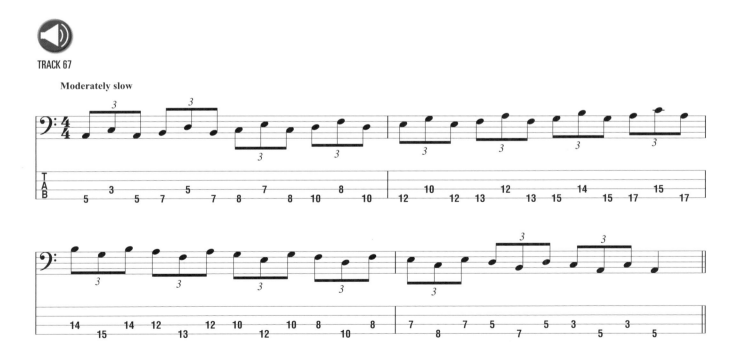

Of course, there are other finger patterns that can be used to play 3rds, as seen in the previous chapters on scales and arpeggios. For a good example of this, refer back to the scale exercise on page 38 (Track 30), which plays through all of the positions of the G major scale in 3rds.

Repetition Is Key

If it seems like some of this material has already been covered in bits and pieces, you're correct. For most musicians with no music theory background, the concept can be extremely confusing and complicated at first, which is why we keep breaking it down into smaller increments and reviewing as we go. It makes more sense to learn the scales and arpeggios first so that we can use them as a guide to understanding their building blocks—the intervals. Instead of bombarding you with way too much detailed information in the first few chapters, we're revisiting the basic concepts and exploring them thoroughly now. If you find yourself getting confused, rather than trying to memorize everything, try your best to understand each individual section as we go. Most students will have a breakthrough at some point and then the big picture will suddenly come into focus.

Oftentimes, bass lines will feature the 3rd transposed an octave lower so that it's played below the root note. Here are the popular finger patterns for playing major and minor 3rds below the root note, with the root notes shown as white circles. For the major 3rd diagram, we've used the note G as the tonic; for the minor 3rd diagram, we've used the note E as the tonic. The two examples that follow are bass lines featuring these intervals.

Major 3rd

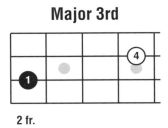

2 fr.

Minor 3rd

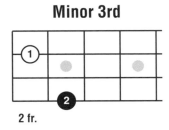

2 fr.

TRACK 68

TRACK 69

68

PERFECT 4THS AND 5THS

As discussed in Chapter 3, 4ths and 5ths are the same distance from the tonic in both major and minor keys. Therefore, these intervals are referred to as *perfect 4ths* and *perfect 5ths*. There is no such thing as a major 4th or minor 4th, or a major 5th or minor 5th.

The perfect 4th interval is two-and-a-half steps above the tonic. On the fretboard, it's located above the tonic at the same fret, one string higher. This is true whether you're in a major or minor key. The diagram below uses D as the tonic, with the perfect 4th, G, shown as a black circle.

Perfect 4th

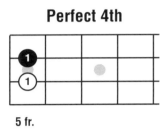

5 fr.

Since the 4th is not a common chord tone, you won't find it used as prominently in bass lines, but there are a few exceptions. It can be very useful as a *passing tone*—a note that is used to connect melodically from one chord tone to the next. The obvious choice would be to connect the 3rd to the 5th, an effect that can be seen in the first example on the previous page (Track 68). Another use for the 4th is to play it against a *suspended 4th* chord (sus4), in which the guitar or piano substitutes the 3rd of the chord with the 4th, then usually resolves the suspended 4th down to the 3rd, causing tension and release. We'll explore these types of chord alterations more in future chapters, but here's a simple example of how the 4th can be used in a bass line against a sus4 chord.

TRACK 70

The perfect 5th is an entirely different story. Because it is a chord tone, and the interval is the same in both major and minor chords, it is hands down the most consonant sounding and commonly used note in bass lines, outside of the tonic and octave. The interval of a perfect 5th is three-and-a-half steps above the tonic. In practice, it is also just as popular to play the perfect 5th below the tonic as it is to play it above the tonic. The following diagrams use E as the tonic and show the location of the perfect 5th (the note B) above it, then below it.

Perfect 5th (above)   Perfect 5th (below)

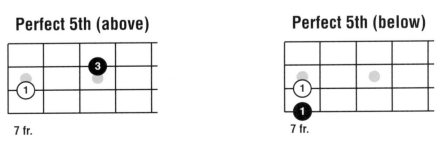

7 fr.   **7 fr.**

Here's a standard groove using only root notes and 5ths. The bass line is played here against a D major chord; however, even if the chord was minor, it would work since the perfect 5th interval is the same in both major and minor chords.

TRACK 71

This next example is played against a chord progression in the key of D minor using 5ths below the root note. This type of bass line will sound familiar to you as well. Notice how easy it is to add in the lower 5ths since they're at the same fret as each of the root notes.

TRACK 72

Here's one more example using 5ths, this time in a 6/8 rhythm. As with the previous examples, you can see how introducing the 5th into the bass line helps to propel the rhythm and make the music a bit more interesting without disturbing the harmonic structure.

TRACK 73

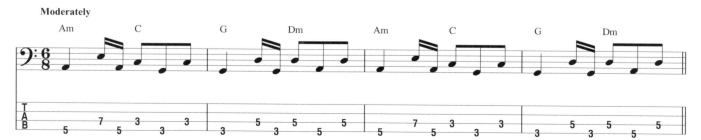

DIMINISHED AND AUGMENTED 4THS AND 5THS

When major 2nds and 3rds are lowered by a half step, they become minor. When perfect 4ths and 5ths are lowered by a half step, they become *diminished*. The concept is the same, but the terminology is different. We can also raise (sharp) 4ths and 5ths by a half step, which will make them *augmented*. For written chord names, special symbols are used to indicate diminished and augmented. For a diminished chord, the "°" symbol is used—for example, C°. For an augmented chord, the "+" symbol is used—for example, C+. You may also encounter music that uses the abbreviations "dim" or "aug" instead, but in this book, we will use symbols.

Diminished and augmented 4ths are rarely used, for a few simple reasons. Since the interval between a major 3rd and a perfect 4th is only a half step, when you flat (diminish) the 4th, the resulting note is enharmonically equivalent to the major 3rd. Similarly, when you sharp (augment) the 4th, it is enharmonically equivalent to the more popular diminished 5th. Still, you will encounter situations where a #4 occurs, mostly in altered major chords.

Diminished and augmented 5ths are much more common, especially the diminished 5th, which is the darkest, most evil-sounding interval in music. In early classical, this interval was banned and referred to as the "Devil's Tritone"—meaning it is three (tri) whole steps (tones) above the tonic. It's no wonder that it is now widely used in heavy metal. Metallica have practically made an entire career out of riffs featuring the diminished 5th. Perhaps the most famous example is the main riff in the song "Black Sabbath," the first track on Black Sabbath's debut album. In triads, the diminished 5th is almost always used in conjunction with a minor 3rd, creating a darker, minor-sounding chord. Here's a diagram showing a common closed-position fingering for the diminished 5th, using the note E as the root note. Below the diagram is an example using the diminished 5th in the context of a metal riff in open position in the key of E minor.

Diminished 5th

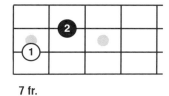

7 fr.

TRACK 74

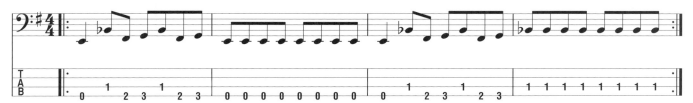

Although they're less common than diminished 5ths, augmented 5ths also occur periodically. Here are two diagrams showing common fingerings for the augmented 5th interval, both using the note E as the root note.

Augmented 5th

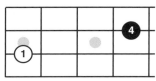

7 fr.

Augmented 5th

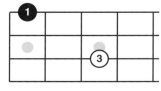

5 fr.

DIMINISHED AND AUGMENTED ARPEGGIOS

In the previous chapter on arpeggios, we took an extensive look at the two most popular R–3–5 triads—major and minor. Now with the introduction of diminished and augmented intervals, we can add diminished and augmented arpeggios to your repertoire. You can use the notes in the diminished and augmented arpeggios to play bass lines against diminished and augmented chords, respectively.

Diminished arpeggios contain a minor 3rd and a diminished 5th. Here are two popular fingerings for the diminished arpeggio, both using the note A at the fifth fret on the fourth string as the root note.

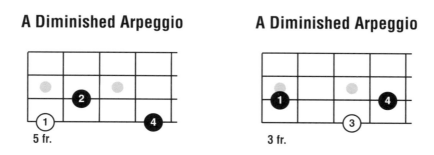

Augmented arpeggios contain a major 3rd and an augmented 5th. Here are two fingerings for the augmented arpeggio, both using the note D at the fifth fret on the third string as the root note.

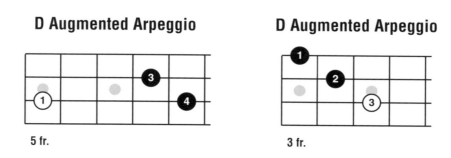

The chart below shows a comprehensive comparison between the four different types of R–3–5 triads. Notice the equal distances between the notes in the diminished and augmented arpeggios. In the augmented arpeggio, the intervals are two whole steps (a major 3rd) between both the root and 3rd and the 3rd and ♯5th. In the diminished arpeggio, the intervals are one-and-a-half steps (a minor 3rd) between both the root and ♭3rd and the ♭3rd and ♭5th. This makes the intervals in the diminished and augmented arpeggios symmetrical.

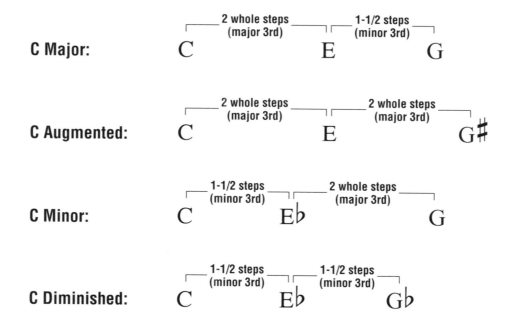

MAJOR AND MINOR 6THS

The 6th step of the major scale is a major 6th above the tonic; the 6th step of the minor scale is a minor 6th above the tonic. The 6ths aren't used as chord tones as often as some of the other intervals; however, when played in the bass register, they can have the effect of inverting the music's harmonic structure and changing the perceived root note of a chord. We will learn more about this later on when we discuss inverted chords.

The major 6th is four-and-a-half steps above the tonic; it's also an inverted minor 3rd (one-and-a-half steps) *below* the tonic's octave. We saw this concept earlier when we discussed relative major and minor keys. Here are a few finger patterns for the major 6th interval, using the note G as the root note, followed by a typical example featuring the major 6th in a bass line.

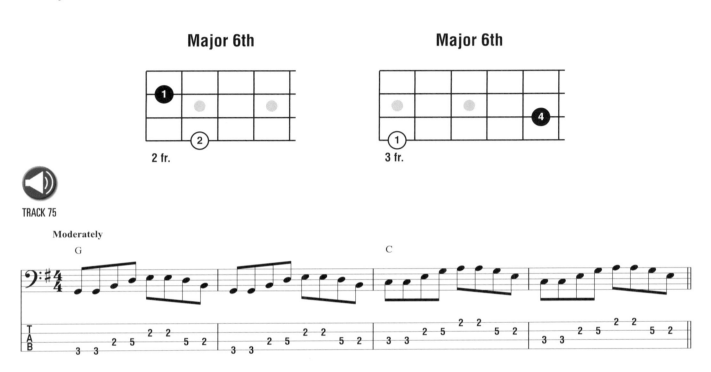

The minor 6th is four whole steps above the tonic, but it is also an inverted major 3rd (two whole steps) *below* the tonic's octave. Here are a few finger patterns for the minor 6th interval, using the note A as the root note, followed by a riff example in the key of F# minor.

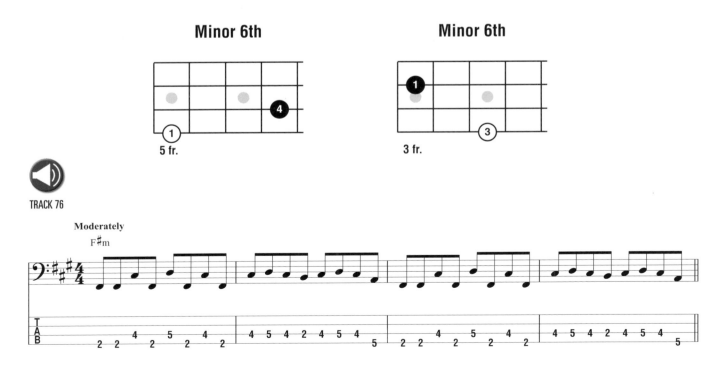

MAJOR, MINOR, AND DIMINISHED 7THS

The 7ths are important intervals because they represent the next most important chord tones above the regular R–3–5 arpeggios. They can be added to major, minor, and diminished chords to lend more color to the harmony. We'll explore this concept and delve into some examples when we examine the different seventh chords later on. Right now, let's focus on where these intervals are located on the fretboard.

In the major scale, the 7th step of the scale is a major 7th, indicated in chord symbols as "maj7." It is also one half step below the octave and is usually referred to as the *leading tone* because it has a very strong tendency to resolve to the tonic, or home. To hear this, simply play through an ascending major scale and stop at the 7th note—the tension created is almost unbearable; it really wants to resolve to the octave!

In the minor scale, the 7th step is a minor 7th, or ♭7, indicated in chord symbols as "m7." The minor 7th interval is one half step lower than the major 7th (or one whole step below the tonic). Minor 7ths are darker and decidedly more bluesy-sounding, depending on the context. They can be added to major, minor, or diminished arpeggios to create a variety of tonal qualities.

The diminished 7th (°7) is where it gets confusing. A diminished 7th is a double-flatted 7th (7) and is one-and-a-half steps lower than the tonic. This is a rule that simply needs to be memorized, since it flies in the face of everything you've learned about intervals so far. The diminished 7th is used in fully diminished seventh chords, which we'll also examine later on. The 7th is most likely the only interval you'll encounter that can be lowered twice in this way. Notice that the 7 is enharmonically equivalent to the major 6th.

The following diagrams show the placement of the 7th intervals, using the note C as the root note.

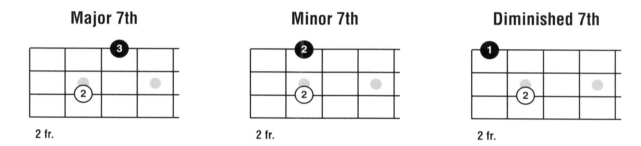

Major 7th	Minor 7th	Diminished 7th
2 fr.	2 fr.	2 fr.

9THS, 10THS, 11THS, AND 13THS

We can also create wider intervals by continuing past the octave. For instance, the 9th is one whole step above the octave, therefore it's the same note as the 2nd played one octave higher. In addition, the 10th is the 3rd played one octave higher, the 11th is the 4th played one octave higher, and the 13th is the 6th played one octave higher. These upper tones are used for *chord extensions*. So far, we've seen that the arpeggios are created by starting on a root note and adding every odd-numbered interval above it (R–3–5). You can continue to add intervals in this way and come up with complex jazz chords that use combinations and variations of the intervals R–3–5–7–9–11–13. When intervals above the octave are altered by a half step, they're usually not referred to as major, minor, diminished, or augmented, but instead employ accidentals within the chord names—for example, ♭9, #9, #11, etc. Here's an example of a bass line using 10ths to outline the major and minor qualities of the chords.

TRACK 77

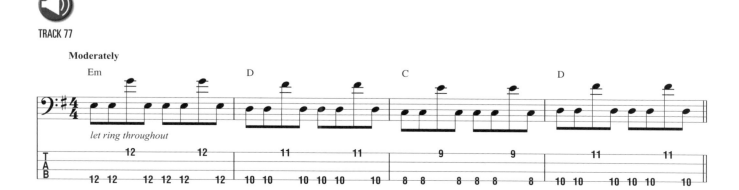

This next example makes good use of the 9th in a bass line in C major. A simpler version of this might have just used 5ths and octaves, but here, the 9th is used instead of the octaves to lend melody to the riffs.

TRACK 78

QUICK REVIEW:

Here's a list of all of the essential intervals within one octave, measured against a C root note and shown in order according to the number of semi-tones (half steps) they are above the tonic:

1.	C to D♭	Minor 2nd
2.	C to D	Major 2nd
3.	C to E♭	Minor 3rd
4.	C to E	Major 3rd
5.	C to F	Perfect 4th
6.	C to F♯	Augmented 4th
	C to G♭	Diminished 5th
7.	C to G	Perfect 5th
8.	C to G♯	Augmented 5th
	C to A♭	Minor 6th
9.	C to A	Major 6th
	C to B	Diminished 7th
10.	C to B♭	Minor 7th
11.	C to B	Major 7th
12.	C to C	Octave

Chapter 8: Pentatonic and Blues Scales

Pentatonic scales are five-note scales that are abbreviated versions of the regular seven-note major and minor scales. Pentatonic scales are the most commonly used scales in rock and blues music. Many bass lines and riffs are based on pentatonic scales, and countless bass players use them for much of their improvisation.

MINOR PENTATONIC SCALES

Arguably, the most frequently used scale in modern rock and popular music is the minor pentatonic scale. It appears in the main riff of many songs, including Aerosmith's "Toys in the Attic," Michael Jackson's "Billie Jean," and countless other songs by bands such as Guns N' Roses. Most riff-based songs are written with the minor pentatonic scale, but it's also the most common go-to scale for bass players to use for fills and riffs. Minor pentatonic utilizes the tonic, 3rd, 4th, 5th, and 7th steps of the natural minor scale.

The A Minor Pentatonic Scale

Let's start out with one of the most useful keys: A minor. The notation, tab, and scale diagram below show one octave of the A minor pentatonic scale, starting at the fifth fret on the fourth string.

The following chart compares the A natural minor scale with the A minor pentatonic scale. By omitting the 2nd and 6th steps of the natural minor scale, we get the notes of the minor pentatonic scale.

	root	2nd	♭3rd	4th	5th	♭6th	♭7th	octave
A Natural Minor:	A	B	C	D	E	F	G	A

	root		♭3rd	4th	5th		♭7th	octave
A Minor Pentatonic:	A		C	D	E		G	A

The following examples show how you can create some very effective bass lines by using just the one-octave minor pentatonic scale. First up is a simple line in A minor that strategically descends the scale. Notice how the five-note pentatonic has a much heavier, primal sound than the melodic-sounding seven-note minor scale.

This next bass line features some grace-note hammer-ons. This one's a little more involved than the previous example but, essentially, it just descends and ascends through the notes of the scale.

Here's another example using the one-octave minor pentatonic scale. This one is played in a shuffle feel and features triplets and some hammer-ons and pull-offs.

The Five Patterns of the A Minor Pentatonic Scale

As with the major and natural minor scales, there are five distinct scale patterns for the minor pentatonic scale, each beginning on a different note of the scale. The first pattern starts with the 1st degree of the scale, the second pattern begins on the 2nd degree of the scale, and so on. Here are the five different scale patterns for the A minor pentatonic scale, beginning with the first pattern, played at the fifth fret.

A Minor Pentatonic Scale: Pattern 1

TRACK 83

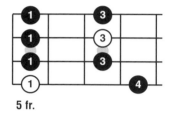

5 fr.

A Minor Pentatonic Scale: Pattern 2

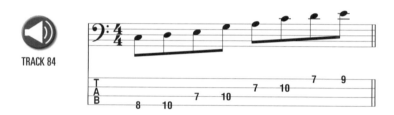

TRACK 84

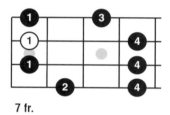

7 fr.

A Minor Pentatonic Scale: Pattern 3

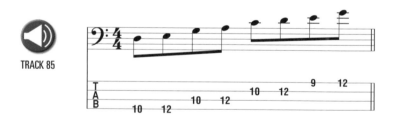

TRACK 85

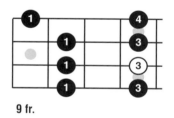

9 fr.

A Minor Pentatonic Scale: Pattern 4

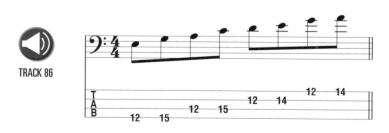

TRACK 86

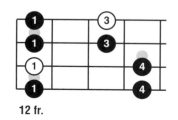

12 fr.

A Minor Pentatonic Scale: Pattern 5

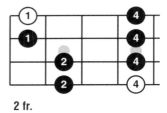

2 fr.

To be thorough, let's also transpose the fourth pattern down an octave to open position. The scale diagram shows the fretted notes played with the second and third fingers. Depending on the context, you can substitute your first and second fingers to fret the notes.

A Minor Pentatonic Scale: Pattern 4 (Open)

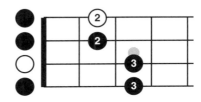

To give you a better sense of how these scale patterns overlap and span the entire fretboard, here's a complete fretboard diagram showing all five patterns. The different patterns are indicated by brackets above and below the fretboard. All of the root notes (A) are indicated with white circles.

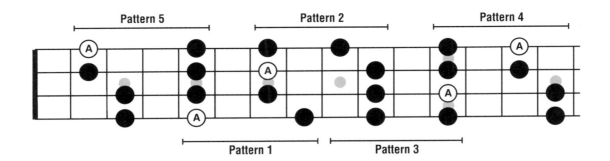

Since each individual pattern contains two notes per string, each pattern has a left side (the lower note on each string) and a right side (the higher note on each string). Notice how the left-side notes of any pattern mirror the right-side notes of the previous pattern.

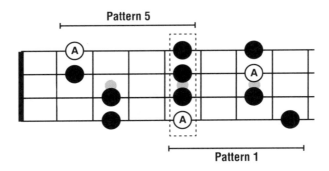

Here are a few examples that span multiple patterns of the A minor pentatonic scale. This first riff travels between the fifth and first patterns.

TRACK 89

The next riff starts all the way up at the 14th fret and shifts through several patterns of the scale before ending up two octaves lower at the fifth fret. Notice how we've used the most comfortable parts of each pattern, only employing the first and third fingers to fret the notes—easy to do with pentatonics.

TRACK 90

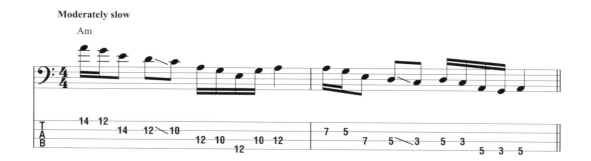

Now let's transpose the minor pentatonic scales to another popular key: E minor. Here are the five scale patterns; the first pattern is shown at both the 12th fret and in open position.

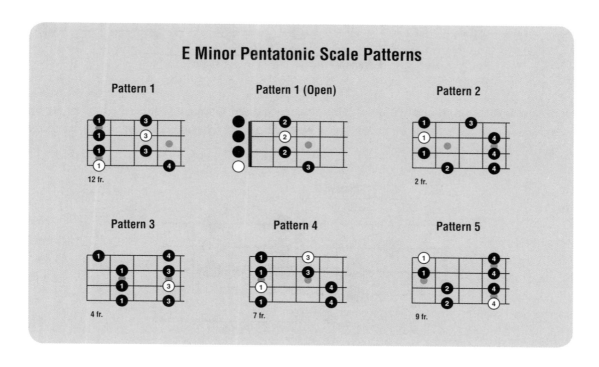

The following E minor pentatonic bass riff effectively employs hammer-ons and pull-offs in open position.

TRACK 91

Moderately slow

Em

This next example starts out with the low open E, but pushes its way up to the fifth fret and seventh fret to utilize parts of the third and fourth patterns.

TRACK 92

Moderately fast

Em

THE BLUES SCALE

The *blues scale* is also very common in rock and blues and can be heard extensively in the catalogs of bands such as Led Zeppelin, Aerosmith, and Guns N' Roses. The scale contains all of the same notes as the minor pentatonic scale, with the addition of the "blues tritone"—the diminished 5th—which is mostly used as a chromatic passing tone between the perfect 4th and perfect 5th. The tonal characteristic of the blues scale is similar to that of the minor pentatonic, but a little sexier, with more personality. Here's one octave of the E blues scale, starting at the seventh fret on the third string.

E Blues Scale

TRACK 93

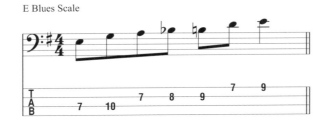

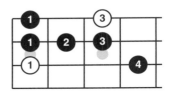

7 fr.

Here's an old-school rock riff utilizing one octave of the E blues scale shown on the previous page. You'll easily recognize the tonal quality of the blues tritone in this example.

TRACK 94

Let's transpose the E blues scale down an octave for this bass line in open position:

TRACK 95

Instead of rehashing every pattern of the pentatonic scale with the blues tritone included, let's take a look at a few places where the note can be conveniently added. With some practice, you'll recognize where the 4th and 5th of the scale are located and where you can slip the tritone between them. Here's the full open-position E blues scale.

TRACK 96

This next passage combines parts of the fifth and first patterns.

TRACK 97

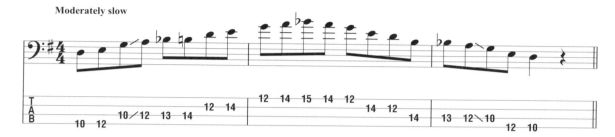

Here's an example that combines parts of the third and fourth patterns.

TRACK 98

The following example combines segments of the different patterns of the E blues scale to create a short solo that spans most of the fretboard. When improvising and playing your own solos, the goal should be to think outside the box and not limit yourself to just one or two areas of the neck.

TRACK 99

83

MAJOR PENTATONIC SCALES

We covered the minor pentatonic scales first in this chapter because they're arguably more popular and used more often than the major pentatonics, especially on the bass. Just like the full major and minor *diatonic* (seven-note) scales, each pentatonic has a relative scale that shares the same notes. The relative keys are determined by the same intervals as the diatonic scales—the tonic of the relative minor is located a 6th above the tonic of its relative major, and conversely, the tonic of the relative major is located a minor 3rd above the tonic of its relative minor. Using this information, we can determine that C is the relative major pentatonic scale of the A minor pentatonic scale. The notes are the same for both scales, the only difference being the location of the tonic. Below is one octave of the C major pentatonic scale. You'll notice that it's closely related to the regular C major scale, but with the 4th and 7th omitted.

C Major Pentatonic Scale

TRACK 100

2 fr.

The following chart compares the notes of the C major scale and the C major pentatonic scale. Just leave out the 4th and 7th for the major pentatonic, and you've got it.

	root	2nd	3rd	4th	5th	6th	7th	octave
C Major:	C	D	E	F	G	A	B	C

	root	2nd	3rd		5th	6th		octave
C Major Pentatonic:	C	D	E		G	A		C

Major pentatonics can be seen everywhere in early rock and walking bass lines. Here's a basic example in the key of C major.

TRACK 101

Moderately fast

C

Let's transpose the scale to a more popular key. Since we already know that G major and E minor are relative keys, it follows that the relative major of the E minor pentatonic scale is the G major pentatonic scale. Therefore, the scale patterns are the same for both except for the location of the root notes. Below are the patterns of the G major pentatonic scale, with all of the root notes (G) shown as white dots.

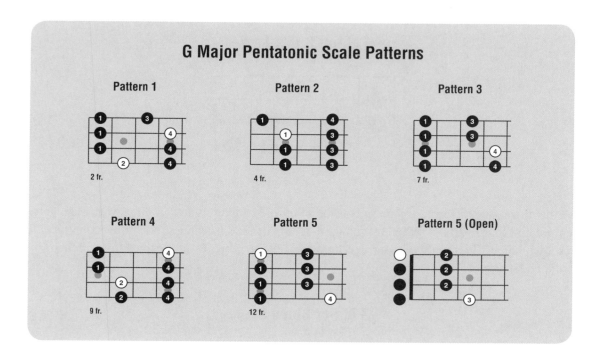

Here's a G major pentatonic example reminiscent of early surf rock.

TRACK 102

Here's another example in G major, this one using the notes of the second pattern. As with the previous two examples, you can see that a "less is more" approach works great with the major pentatonics.

TRACK 103

THE MAJOR BLUES SCALE

There's a major version of the blues scale, too, that incorporates a chromatic passing tone between the 2nd and 3rd. This keeps the integrity of the relative major and minor keys intact, with both relative scales containing the exact same notes. Here's one octave of the G major blues scale, starting at the third fret on the fourth string.

G Major Blues Scale

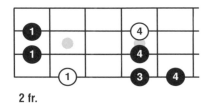

2 fr.

You'll notice that the above fingering is a bit uncomfortable, since the three-note chromatic passage gets split up between the third and fourth strings. When using the scale for riffs and bass lines, it's more economical to shift positions as shown below. Start out with your first finger on the root note, G, at the third fret and then slide up two frets to play the rest of the scale.

G Major Blues Scale

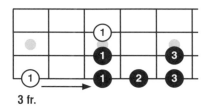

3 fr.

Here's an example of a bass riff using the above G major blues scale fingering.

TRACK 104

The major blues scale works really well in open keys. Here's one octave of the A major blues scale starting with the open third string.

A Major Blues Scale

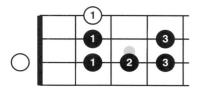

Here's an example in the key of A using the open major blues scale. Parts of it are reminiscent of the main riff of the Beatles' "Day Tripper."

TRACK 105

Let's transpose the scale once again, this time to the key of E major. The following solo incorporates many different positions of the E major pentatonic and E major blues scales.

TRACK 106

SCALE AND ARPEGGIO COMPARISONS

The following chart reviews how the major and minor pentatonic scales and the major and minor arpeggios are derived from the regular major and minor diatonic scales by simply subtracting some of the notes. If you haven't recognized how these arpeggios and scales relate to each other yet, this clear series of fretboard diagrams should help.

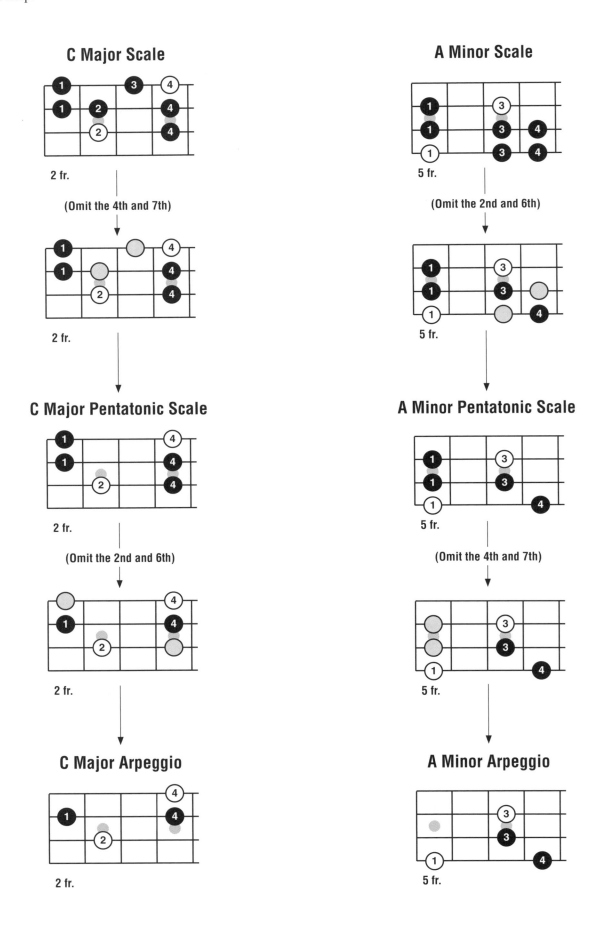

Breaking the Rules

It's important to learn the rules before you break them, but the use of pentatonic and blues scales doesn't need to strictly adhere to major and minor all of the time. The minor pentatonic and blues scales can often be used in a major key, too. You'll clearly hear this in the guitar solos of blues masters Buddy Guy, Stevie Ray Vaughan, and Eric Clapton. On the bass, it's evident with players like Duff McKagan. Bass players often tend to favor the minor pentatonic even when they're playing in a major key. Sometimes it works great, sometimes it doesn't; use your ear and feel your way through it. In addition, you can substitute or add notes to the scales. In major pentatonic, the addition of the ♭7 (borrowed from the minor pentatonic) sounds great and adds a blues flavor to the scale. You can also experiment with other chromatic passing tones instead of limiting yourself to just the blues tritone. Learn the scales first, then follow your instincts and see what works.

QUICK REVIEW:

- Pentatonic scales are five-note scales that are abbreviated versions of the regular seven-note major and minor scales.

- The intervals contained in the minor pentatonic scale are the root, ♭3rd, 4th, 5th, and ♭7th.

- The blues scale is a variation of the minor pentatonic scale that incorporates a ♭5th, called the "blues tritone," as a chromatic passing tone between the 4th and 5th of the scale.

- The intervals contained in the major pentatonic scale are the root, 2nd, 3rd, 5th, and 6th.

- The major blues scale is a variation of the major pentatonic scale that incorporates a chromatic passing tone between the 2nd and 3rd of the scale.

Chapter 9: Harmonizing the Scales

In previous chapters, we learned how to determine the notes in an arpeggio or chord by stacking 3rds—adding every other note of the scale above any particular root note to get its correct 3rd and 5th. If we harmonize an entire scale by building a triad on each note, we'll come up with a series of chords, one for each step of the scale. These chords represent the basic chords used to create chord progressions in that particular key.

HARMONIZING THE MAJOR SCALE

Let's begin with our trusty C major scale since it contains all natural notes. If we add the 3rd and 5th above every step of the scale, we'll get all of the chords in the key of C major. Some chords will be major, some will be minor, depending on the particular intervals created above each individual root note. Here's the harmonized scale shown in music notation with the chord names indicated above the staff. Notice that the chords built on the tonic, 4th, and 5th are major chords. All of the rest are minor chords, with the exception of the 7th, which is a diminished chord. This information is true for every major key.

In music theory analysis, Roman numerals are used to indicate the types of chords. Uppercase Roman numerals refer to major chords, while lowercase Roman numerals refer to minor chords. The 3rd of each chord determines whether it's a major or minor chord.

Here is a chart of all the basic three-note chords in the key of C major, in order, with the Roman-numeral analysis indicated above the chord names. This series of Roman numerals gives us a consistent formula that can be applied to any other major key, and the order and quality of the chords will remain the same—the I chord is always major, the ii chord is always minor, and so on.

I	ii	iii	IV	V	vi	vii°
C	**Dm**	**Em**	**F**	**G**	**Am**	**B°**
major	minor	minor	major	major	minor	diminished

The scale degrees (and the triads that are built on them) also have theoretical names that can be used to refer to them:

1. **Tonic:** Home (the same as the name of the key).

2. **Supertonic:** 2nd degree (the note directly above the tonic).

3. **Mediant:** 3rd degree (the middle note between the tonic and the dominant).

4. **Subdominant:** 4th degree (also the distance of a perfect 5th *below* the tonic, hence the term *sub*dominant).

5. **Dominant:** 5th degree (the most dominant note besides the tonic—the distance of a perfect 5th *above* the tonic).

6. **Submediant:** 6th degree (the middle note between the tonic and the subdominant below the tonic, hence the term *sub*mediant).

7. **Leading tone:** 7th degree (the note that leads to the tonic, sometimes referred to as the "subtonic").

Using the notes in the first pattern of the C major scale, here are all of the arpeggios in the key of C major in order—first ascending, then descending.

TRACK 107

Now let's transpose the chords to the next key in the Circle of 5ths: G major. As you can see, the order of the major- and minor-type chords remains the same.

I	ii	iii	IV	V	vi	vii°
G	**A**	**B**	**C**	**D**	**E**	**F♯°**
major	minor	minor	major	major	minor	diminished

Here's an exercise using all of the arpeggios in G major. For this one, play only the arpeggio patterns that begin with the second finger, progressing up the fretboard in a linear fashion, then back down.

TRACK 108

HARMONIZING THE MINOR SCALE

You can also build chords in minor keys by harmonizing each step of the minor scale. Here are the chords in the key of A minor with the corresponding Roman-numeral analysis indicated above.

i	ii°	III	iv	v	VI	VII
Am	**B°**	**C**	**Dm**	**Em**	**F**	**G**
minor	diminished	major	minor	minor	major	major

Now that you have the formula for the harmonized minor scale, you can easily transpose it to other keys as well. Here are the chords in the key of B minor.

i	ii°	III	iv	v	VI	VII
Bm	**C♯°**	**D**	**Em**	**F♯m**	**G**	**A**
minor	diminished	major	minor	minor	major	major

For this next exercise, in the key of B minor, play only the arpeggio patterns that begin with the first finger, ascending and descending the fretboard like the example on the previous page. While these exercises work great as a warm-up, they can also help you to memorize the order and quality of the chords in each key.

TRACK 109

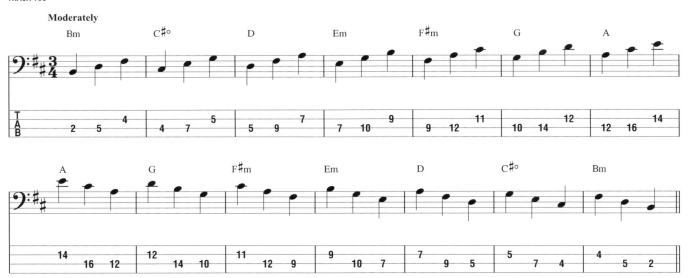

Here is the order of the chord types in the major and minor keys, shown only with Roman numerals. Remember: these formulas hold true for all major or minor keys, no matter what the tonic is.

Major Keys

major	minor	minor	major	major	minor	diminished
I	ii	iii	IV	V	vi	vii°

Minor Keys

minor	diminished	major	minor	minor	major	major
i	ii°	III	iv	v	VI	VII

At this point, you'll probably begin to recognize familiar patterns between major and minor with respect to the order in which the chords are arranged. This is due to the relative major and minor phenomenon. Although the order of chords by quality (major, minor, or diminished) remains consistent, the tonic is different, therefore the Roman numerals for the rest of the chords change in relation to it. The following chart may help to clarify this concept; it shows all of the chords in the key of A minor, with the chords in the relative key of C major below them. Notice that both keys contain all of the same letter-name chords, and the chord that functions as the tonic (i chord or I chord) is what establishes the key and tonal center.

i	ii°	III	iv	v	VI	VII		
Am	**B°**	**C**	**Dm**	**Em**	**F**	**G**		
minor	diminished	major	minor	minor	major	major		

	I	ii	iii	IV	V	vi	vii°
	C	**Dm**	**Em**	**F**	**G**	**Am**	**B°**
	major	minor	minor	major	major	minor	diminished

Learning Roman-Numeral Analysis Is Essential

This is what everything you've learned so far has led up to. Chord analysis is what music theory is all about, and once you have an understanding of the concept of Roman-numeral analysis, it will unlock endless potential. The Roman numerals are used to describe *chord progressions*—the series and order of chords in relation to each other in a song—independent of what the key is. For example, you may be asked to play a I–IV–V progression in C major, which means the chords are the I chord (C), the IV chord (F), and the V chord (G). However, you may also need to play the same I–IV–V progression in B♭ major for a different song, and if you know how to find the I, IV, and V chords in B♭ major on the fretboard, you're all set!

There are numerous reasons why this knowledge is essential, one obvious reason being the ability to transpose chord progressions and songs to other keys. Another important reason is that so many songs are based on standard chord progressions (for example, the very popular I–IV–V mentioned above), and you'll often be playing against the same progressions from song to song, even when the keys are different. In fact, hundreds of popular songs use the exact same progressions. This knowledge is what you'll need to take your playing to the next level. Many musicians get comfortable playing in particular keys (such as E, A, or G), but once you're able to recognize popular chord progressions, you'll be able to play with ease in just about any key. We're going to dive into playing bass lines in many popular chord progressions in the next chapter, so make sure you have this information down first.

SEVENTH CHORDS

We can extend triads one more chord tone by stacking an additional 3rd on top of them, giving us the seventh chords. Adding the 7th brings more color to the tonal quality of a chord. Some seventh chords are used more often than others, depending on the style of music. There are four main types of seventh chords found in major and minor keys: major seventh (maj7), minor seventh (m7), dominant seventh (7), and minor seventh flat-five (m7♭5). The diagrams below show the most comfortable arpeggio fingerings for the four types of seventh chords, each using the note A as the root note. Remember: these finger patterns are moveable on the bass and can be transposed.

A Major Seventh

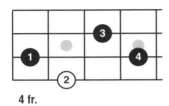

4 fr.

A Minor Seventh

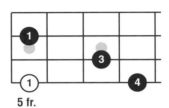

5 fr.

A Dominant Seventh

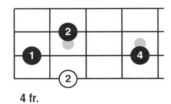

4 fr.

A Minor Seventh Flat-Five

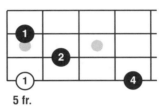

5 fr.

Here are a few examples that demonstrate the tonal quality of some of the popular seventh chords. This first bass line uses all minor seventh arpeggios, repeating the same pattern for each chord. Notice how similar the minor seventh arpeggio is to the minor pentatonic scale (the arpeggio contains four of the pentatonic scale's five notes).

TRACK 110

94

This next example is a walking-bass pattern using all dominant seventh chords. In addition to the notes of the arpeggios, the 6th of each chord is included as a passing tone. This popular bass line should sound very familiar to you.

TRACK 111

We can harmonize the major scale with all seventh chords the same way we harmonized the scale with triads. Each step of the major scale yields a specific seventh chord.

Here's an exercise that progresses through all of the seventh-chord arpeggios in the key of C major. It begins on the Cmaj7 arpeggio, with the root note on the third string at the third fret, then moves up the fretboard one arpeggio at a time until it reaches the octave at the 15th fret. This exercise will help you memorize which seventh chord is used for each step of the major scale. In future chapters, we'll utilize these seventh-chord arpeggios in more musical applications.

TRACK 112

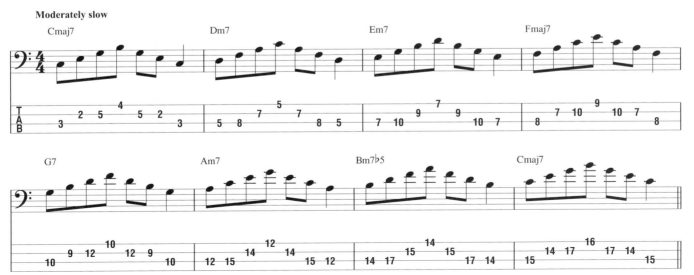

REVIEW QUIZ

Name the arpeggios in the following fretboard diagrams. Answers at the bottom of the page.

1.

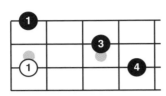

7 fr.

2.

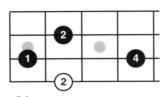

5 fr.

3.

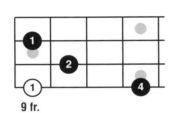

9 fr.

4.

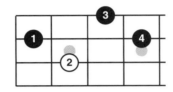

4 fr.

5. List the triads in the key of D minor.

6. List the triads in the key of F♯ major.

7. List the seventh chords in the key of E major.

8. List the seventh chords in the key of B♭ major.

Chapter 10: Chord Progressions

In this chapter, we'll explore some of the most popular chord progressions and show you how to analyze and identify them in any key. Learning the basic theory behind these progressions will help demystify song structure and lay the groundwork you'll use for improvising and creating bass lines. We'll be using a lot of Roman-numeral analysis and chord formulas from the previous chapter, so if you don't have them down yet, take a minute to review the rules before moving on.

MAJOR CHORD PROGRESSIONS

Let's begin by exploring some of the most common chord progressions used in major keys.

I–IV–V

The I–IV–V progression is a classic that's been used since the early days of rock music, and it's still used in many songs today. Most blues songs are based on a I–IV–V progression. Here's an example in the key of G major. The bass line uses the notes of the major pentatonic scale for each chord to create a popular riff-based line that's reminiscent of early rock 'n' roll.

TRACK 113

When we discussed intervals, scales, and arpeggios in previous chapters, we used moveable fretboard diagrams to show how you can visualize these patterns and apply them on the bass. The same can be done with chord progressions, making them easier to visualize and transpose to other keys. Here are a few versions of the I–IV–V progression in G major using Roman numerals to indicate the location of the root notes for each chord. The tonic is indicated with a white circle in each. The first diagram shows the tonic as the lowest note, at the third fret on the fourth string; the second diagram shows the tonic as the highest note, at the fifth fret on the second string.

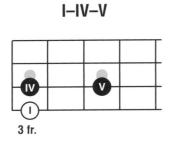

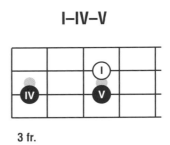

It's not unusual to switch up the order of the I–IV–V progression a little and alter the duration of the chords. Here's an example in the key of D major.

TRACK 114

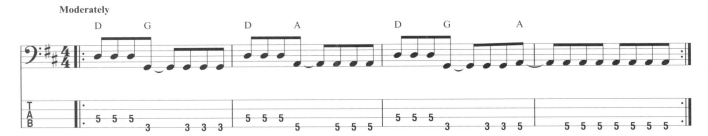

Here's a I–IV–V example in E major that also includes the minor 3rd (the note G) from the minor pentatonic scale to give the progression a heavier sound. This is reminiscent of the Joan Jett song "I Love Rock 'n' Roll."

TRACK 115

I–♭VII–IV

Here's another popular three-chord progression that's often used in major keys: I–♭VII–IV. By lowering the root note of the seventh chord one half step, it becomes a major chord. On the fretboard, this progression looks a lot like the I–IV–V progression. It's basically taking the I, IV, and V chords and switching the order around so that, in context, the V chord now functions as the tonic (I chord). The following example is a I–♭VII–IV progression in the key of E major.

TRACK 116

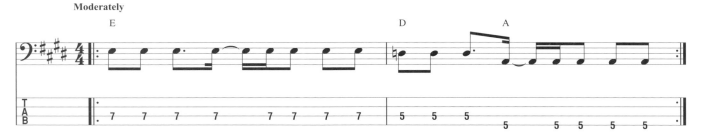

Here's what the I–♭VII–IV progression looks like on the fretboard in the key of E. Note the similarity to the I–IV–V progression—the only difference being which chord functions as the tonic.

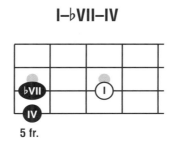

I–♭VII–IV

5 fr.

I–V–vi–IV

This four-chord progression is one of the most commonly used major-key progressions in modern rock and pop music. You'll recognize this from thousands of popular songs, so it's important for you to be able to play it in different keys and with the tonic in different octaves. This first example is in the key of C major.

TRACK 117

Moderately

The I–V–vi–IV progression is another good one to depict using fretboard diagrams. Two versions are shown below in C major, one with the tonic played above the other chords, and one with the tonic played below them.

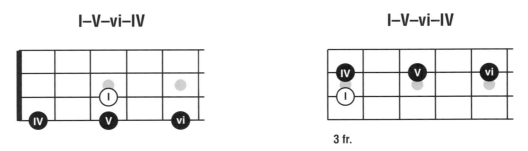

I–V–vi–IV   **I–V–vi–IV**

3 fr.

Here's another example of the I–V–vi–IV progression. This one is in 6/8 time and the key of F major, with the root of the I chord (F) as the lowest note in the bass line.

TRACK 118

Moderately slow

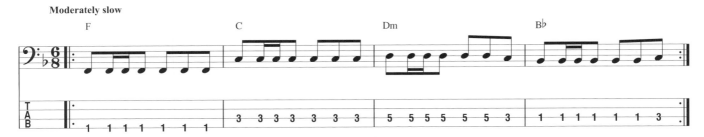

IV–I–V–vi

This popular progression is a slight variation of the previous one. It uses the same chords in the same order, but the progression starts on the IV chord instead of the I chord. This example is in the key of A major, with the bass playing low E and low F♯ for the V and vi chords, respectively.

TRACK 119

I–V–vi

Here's a three-chord variation of the previous progression that leaves off the IV chord entirely. The following bass line—also in A major—is similar to "Jailbreak" by Thin Lizzy.

TRACK 120

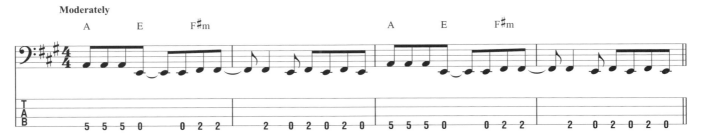

I–V–ii–IV

This progression is also similar to the I–V–vi–IV progression; we've simply substituted the vi chord with the ii chord. Here's the progression in the key of G major.

TRACK 121

Here's the I–V–ii–IV progression in the key of G shown with a fretboard diagram. You'll most likely see the root notes of the chords in this array, but remember that any of them can be transposed to a different octave.

I–V–ii–IV

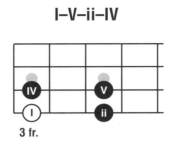

3 fr.

I–V–iii–IV

Now let's take the above progression and substitute the iii chord for the ii chord. This is a popular move in modern rock songs from the '90s. The tonic, G, is played above the other chords in the first part of the example, then played below the other chords for the second part.

TRACK 122

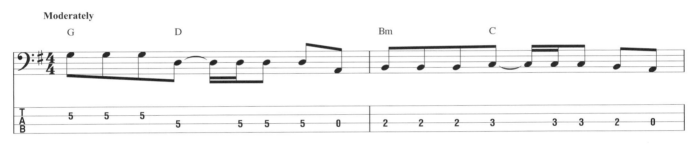

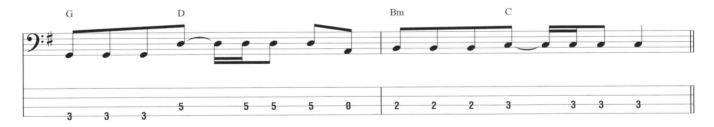

Here are two diagrams that correspond with the above I–V–iii–IV example in G major, showing the tonic in both the higher and lower octaves.

I–V–iii–IV

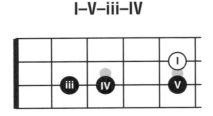

I–V–iii–IV

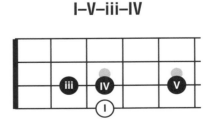

MINOR CHORD PROGRESSIONS

Let's explore some of the popular chord progressions in minor keys. At this point, you'll probably begin to recognize familiar patterns in the order in which the chords are arranged. Some of these minor progressions will use the same chords as the major progressions; however, the tonic (i chord) is what establishes the minor key and determines the Roman-numeral analysis.

i–VI–VII–i

Our first minor progression is the most popular go-to chord progression for many heavy metal and hard rock songs. Here it is in the key of A minor, played over a typical rock beat.

TRACK 123

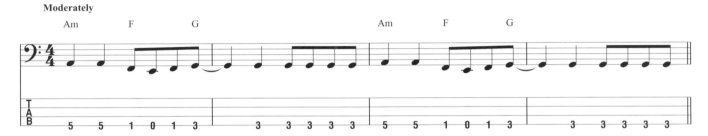

An interesting theoretical observation can be made about the above progression. The key of A minor's relative major is C major, and the most popular major key progression is the I–IV–V. In C major, those chords are C, F, and G. Here, in the relative minor key, we have the most popular minor progression (i–VI–VII) containing the chords Am, F, and G. The only difference between the two progressions is that, in the minor key, we're using the Am chord as the tonic; the other two chords (F and G) are the same in both keys. Since Roman-numeral analysis is determined by the other chords' relationship to the tonic, the numerals are different, but the chords are exactly the same. We've basically just taken a I–IV–V major progression, dumped the major tonic and replaced it with its relative minor tonic. Here's a fretboard diagram showing the progression in the key of A minor.

i–VI–VII–i

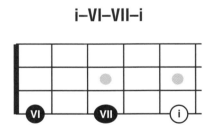

The next example features the same i–VI–VII–i progression, this time in the key of E minor, with a popular metal rhythm reminiscent of many songs by Iron Maiden.

TRACK 124

i–VI

Oftentimes, you'll encounter a simplified version of the previous progression using just the i and VI chords. Here's an example in E minor.

TRACK 125

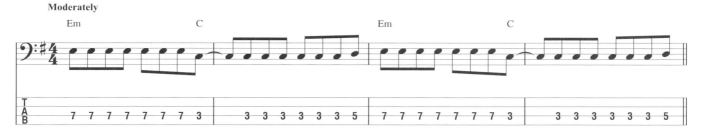

Many of the progressions in this section are shown in the popular key of E minor, making it easier for you to compare them and recognize their differences. E minor is often used in rock in order to utilize the low open E string for the tonic. Here's the previous progression transposed to F♯ minor, which is another popular minor key. For this example, the tonic is played in the lower octave, with the VI chord played above it. This is also depicted in the fretboard diagram below.

TRACK 126

i–VI

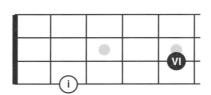

i–VI–VII–v

Here's a variation of the previous progression that introduces a minor v chord to the mix.

TRACK 127

i–VII–VI–V

Sometimes it's preferable to alter the minor v chord to make it a major V chord instead. This is a common practice that was co-opted from early classical music, when chords in minor keys were often built on a *harmonic minor scale* (a minor scale with a raised 7th). We'll delve into the theory behind the harmonic minor and other altered minor scales in detail later on. The progression featured here can be heard in the chorus of "N.I.B." by Black Sabbath.

TRACK 128

i–VI–iv–VII

This progression is a variation of the i–VI–VII that inserts a minor iv chord into the mix.

TRACK 129

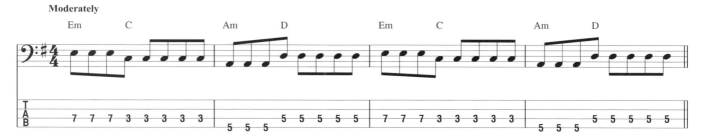

Here's the i–VI–iv–VII progression as a fretboard diagram in the key of E minor.

I–VI–iv–VII

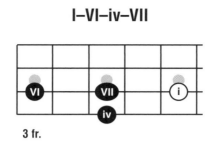

3 fr.

i–VI–III–VII

The use of the major III chord is also common in minor-key progressions. This progression is the same as the previous one, except that we've substituted the iv chord (Am) with the III chord (G). The progression is also shown below as a fretboard diagram; compare it with the diagram above and note the similarities.

TRACK 130

I–VI–III–VII

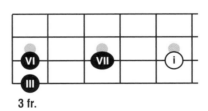

3 fr.

i–VII–III–VI

The previous progression works just as well if you switch the order of the chords around. In this case, we've opted to play the note G an octave higher in the bass line.

TRACK 131

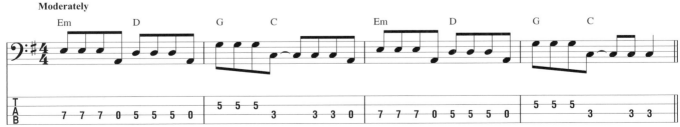

i–III–VII–VI

Let's vary the order of the chords again, this time placing the III chord (G) second in the progression.

TRACK 132

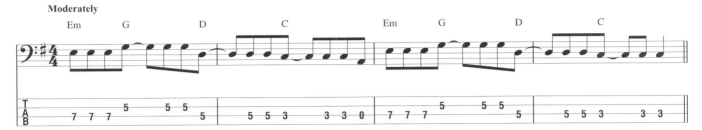

i–III–VII–iv

Now let's take the previous progression and substitute the VI chord (C) with the iv chord (Am). To make things a little more interesting, we've thrown in some scale tones to show you how a bass melody will work against this progression. When each chord in the progression changes, the bass plays the root note of the chord, anchoring the harmonic structure within the melody.

TRACK 133

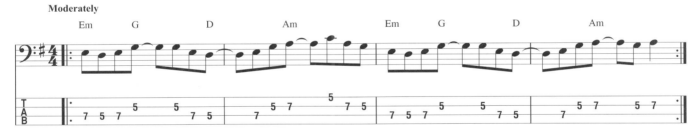

The following fretboard diagram corresponds to the above i–III–VII–iv progression in E minor, showing where the root notes of each chord are played in the example. Remember: all of these root notes can be transposed to other octaves to alter the pattern.

I–III–VII–iv

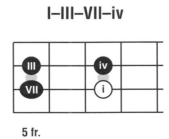

5 fr.

TRADITIONAL CHORD SEQUENCES

Harmonic progressions in early classical music established certain consonant chord sequences that remain somewhat common in popular music today. Of course, these rules are often broken and altered, just like all other rules of music theory, but examining these chord sequences will give you some reference points to help understand how typical modern progressions function and why.

Let's examine the chords in major keys and how they function in relation to each other. From the I chord (the tonic), you can basically jump to any other chord in the key. The concern is not so much where you go from I, but how you get back to I—which chords and what order will take you back smoothly to the tonic. It's been established that the V chord (dominant) has the strongest pull back to the tonic. The V–I chord sequence will often occur at the end of a piece of music, or at the end of a complete section within a piece. This is also referred to as a V–I *cadence* because it resolves back to home.

$$V \longrightarrow I$$

If we move backwards from the V chord in the Circle of 5ths, we can add the ii chord (supertonic) before it.

$$ii \longrightarrow V \longrightarrow I$$

Going backwards in the Circle of 5ths from the ii chord gives us the vi chord (submediant).

$$vi \longrightarrow ii \longrightarrow V \longrightarrow I$$

Another 5th backwards gives us the iii chord, which is pretty far removed from the tonic in the sequence.

$$iii \longrightarrow vi \longrightarrow ii \longrightarrow V \longrightarrow I$$

At this point, you may be wondering where the IV chord is. The IV (subdominant) was often substituted for the ii chord in these cycles. Let's compare the two chords in the key of C major. The ii chord is a Dm chord (D–F–A), and the IV chord is F (F–A–C), so you can see how similar they are with respect to the notes contained in both chords.

$$iii \longrightarrow vi \longrightarrow IV \longrightarrow V \longrightarrow I$$

Another common move you might see is when the V chord resolves to the vi chord, instead of the I chord. This is what's known as a *deceptive cadence* and is used as a device to avoid the predictable habit of following the V with the tonic. A deceptive cadence can move you backwards in the progression to the submediant, taking the music in a different direction, and it can also be used to modulate to the relative minor or to other keys.

$$iii \longrightarrow vi \longrightarrow IV \longrightarrow V \longrightarrow vi$$

You'll see bits and pieces of the above chord sequences in modern popular music, but remember that these rules are hundreds of years old and come from a structured genre established early in the history of music. If you examine the previous progressions in this chapter, you'll probably recognize how some of those sequences are variations of these traditional harmonic progressions.

ANALYZING AND TRANSPOSING PROGRESSIONS

If you paid close attention to the fretboard patterns we used to identify the chord progressions in the previous section, transposing them on the bass should be a snap, just like transposing scales and arpeggios. There are some other essential tools to equip yourself with—most importantly, how to determine the key of a song.

Determining the Key

Once your ear is sufficiently trained and you begin to hear familiar patterns in chord progressions, riffs, and scales, identifying the key of a song should come naturally to you in most instances. More often than not, a song will start and/or end on the I chord, but that's not always a set rule for decisively determining the key. Many progressions have a natural pull that wants to resolve home to the tonic. The most popular occurrences of this happen in a V–I or a ii–V–I chord change. These specific instances are referred to as *cadences* and usually happen as part of a longer progression or series of chords. In any event, they have such a strong sonic resolution to the tonic that your ear will easily recognize which chord is supposed to be I.

If you're given written music that includes a key signature, you can already narrow down the key to two possibilities: the major key or its relative minor. For example, the following selection's key signature has three sharps, so the music will either be in the key of A major or the key of F# minor.

TRACK 134

The key in the above example should be pretty obvious. It starts and ends on an A chord, but also notice the absence of any F#m chords. Without the presence of an F#m, it can't possibly be in the key of F# minor since there is no minor tonic (F#m chord) to be found. We can also confirm a major key cadence by analyzing the progression. If A is the tonic (I), then D is the IV chord, Bm is the ii chord, and E is the V chord. Therefore, the last three chords represent a ii–V–I cadence.

Let's take a look at another example, this one with a key signature of two sharps, putting it in the key of D major or B minor.

TRACK 135

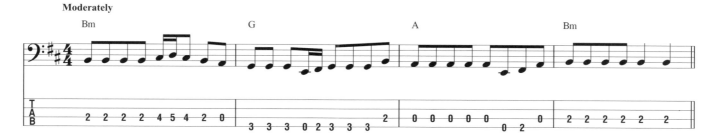

The key of the previous example is also pretty obvious. It starts on a Bm chord and definitively resolves back to the Bm chord at the end of the example, making Bm the obvious choice for the tonic. There are also no D chords present, so it couldn't possibly be in the key of D major. The chord progression is therefore the popular i–VI–VII–i minor progression.

Figuring out the keys for the last two bass lines was pretty easy, since you were lucky enough to have the written music giving you the key signature. This significantly narrows down the possibilities. But what if you don't have the music? What if you only have a chord chart, or if you are figuring out the song by ear? At this point, you may also be wondering why it's so important to even know what key the song is in; why not just play the notes without worrying about it? Well, knowing the key of the song will tell you what scales you can use to improvise or craft your own bass parts. Furthermore, you'll be able to determine which arpeggios you can play against the chords.

Let's take a look at a simple chord chart. There's no key signature to give you clues; you just have to go by the information presented—the chords, chord types, and order of the chords.

The first clue is that most of the chords are major, the only exception being the A minor chord, which occurs in the middle of the progression. We can safely determine this is a major key. The second clue is that the progression starts on a G major chord and resolves at the end to the G major chord, which you can clearly hear on the rhythm track. If we assume the progression is in the key of G major, let's call G the tonic (I) and then label the chords by Roman numeral:

```
   I      V      ii     IV     I      V      ii     IV     I
   G      D     |Am     C     |G      D     |Am     C     |G          ||
```

We can clearly see that this is the familiar I–V–ii–IV progression we studied earlier in the chapter. Let's try another one:

This one isn't quite as obvious as it appears to be. We can assume it's in a major key since there are no minor chords, but the order of the chords might trip you up. If you play the notes on the bass, it will look like the familiar I–IV–V chords in the key of G major. This is incorrect, though! The progression clearly starts on D, ends on D, and always resolves to D—the G chord doesn't sound like home at all. The tonic is so obviously D that we have to go with our I–♭VII–IV–I progression in the key of D major. This progression is famously heard in "Sweet Child O' Mine" by Guns N' Roses, as well as countless other songs in many different keys.

```
       I                ♭VII              IV               I
       D                |C                |G               |D          ||
```

Here's another example that contains a few minor chords. Listen to the track and use your ear to identify the tonic.

TRACK 138   Em   C |Am   D |Em   C |Am   D |Em ||

It seems to resolve quite well to the Em chord, and it also starts on Em. If we assume it's in the key of E minor, and we assign Roman numerals to the chords in relation to the tonic, we come up with another chord progression from earlier in the chapter: i–VI–iv–VII.

          i   VI   iv   VII   i   VI   iv   VII   i

          Em   C |Am   D |Em   C |Am   D |Em ||

Let's say you don't have a chord chart, and you're figuring out a song by ear. You've managed to pick out the root notes of each chord so far. At this point, your ear should be developed enough to hear the difference between major and minor chords. But what if they're neither major or minor? What if you're dealing with simple power chords (a root and 5th in the chord with no 3rd)? Let's take a look at the example below, which consists of all power chords.

TRACK 139   E5   G5 |A5   C5   D5 |E5   G5 |A5   C5   D5 |E5 ||

It does sound like the E5 chord is home—it starts on E and resolves to E at the end. But how can you tell if it's major or minor? Simple deduction. The key of E major has four sharps: F#, G#, C#, and D#, but there are G5, C5, and D5 chords present and none of them are sharped. However, the key of E minor only has one sharp, F#, and all the rest of the notes are natural notes. The rest of the chords fit into this narrative, so even though none of them are major or minor, the context of the root notes tells you that the key must be E minor. Here's the analysis, expanded to indicate major or minor in context according to the harmony implied by the key of E minor. This is a good exercise to get into because, even though the guitarist is only playing power chords, if you want to play arpeggios, you'll know which ones work against the chords.

          i   III   iv   VI   VII   i   III   iv   VI   VII   i

          E5   G5 |A5   C5   D5 |E5   G5 |A5   C5   D5 |E5 ||

REVIEW QUIZ

Name the chords for each of the following progressions in the indicated key. You can refer back to the chapter examples for clues, use your knowledge of the fretboard, and refer to the major and minor scales to figure out the root notes. Answer key is at the bottom of the page.

1. **I–V–vi–IV in the key of A major.**

2. **I–IV–V in the key of E♭ major.**

3. **I–♭VII–IV in the key of F major.**

4. **I–V–ii–IV in the key of B major.**

5. **i–VI–VII–i in the key of F♯ minor.**

6. **i–III–VII–iv in the key of D minor.**

7. **i–VI–iv–VII in the key of A minor.**

8. **i–VII–III–VI in the key of G minor.**

Chapter 11: Inversions

When a chord is played with the root note as the lowest-sounding tone (or "in the bass"), it is said to be in *root position*. If we transpose the root note to a higher octave so that the 3rd is now the lowest-sounding tone, the chord will be in *first inversion*. If we play the same chord but with the 5th as the lowest-sounding tone, it will be in *second inversion*. Since the bass is almost always the lowest-pitched instrument in a band or ensemble, bass players can create chord inversions in the music by playing the 3rd or the 5th of the arpeggio instead of the root note. This presents a unique opportunity for the bass player to invert the overall tonal quality of the music. Use this power wisely and with taste, and don't overdo it! The low frequencies of the bass guitar have a huge impact when playing the 3rd or 5th below the rest of the band. If it doesn't work, the people you're playing with will be sure to shoot you some sour looks, or they'll tell you that you're hitting the wrong note; if you pull it off right, they'll praise you for how amazing it sounds.

FIRST INVERSION

Putting a chord in first inversion is a great device for injecting melody into your playing. In the previous chapter on chord progressions, we noticed that many chord changes happen in cycles of 4ths and 5ths. If you only play root notes, the bass line will tend to have a lot of wide interval jumps. A few carefully placed 3rds in the bass will create a more melodic part and can improve the contour of the bass line. Paul McCartney was a master of this technique.

Let's take a look at a basic example. The bass line below runs through a simple chord progression three times so you can hear the difference. The inversions are indicated in the chord analysis above the staff using slashed chord symbols. For example, the chord symbol D/F# indicates that the chord is D major, but the bass is playing F# (the 3rd of the D major chord). The first time through the progression, the bass plays all root notes. The second time, the bass tastefully substitutes 3rds for a few of the chords, creating a logical, descending melody. The third time, we tried something different by inverting the last chord of each phrase. The bass looks OK on its own because it's playing a basic root-5th figure; however, it isn't as preferable because the last note of each phrase just sounds wrong for a few reasons. The inversions aren't being used there to create anything melodic, and using an inversion at the end of a phrase leaves it sounding unresolved. Of course, that's a matter of taste, and nothing says that you can't break the rules, so experiment as much as you want. Let your ear dictate what you think sounds good.

TRACK 140

112

Let's take a look at another one. This is a variation of a basic I–IV–V progression in E major, but we've put one of the E chords in first inversion, giving this simple chord change some new life. This example is reminiscent of the verses in "The Spirit of Radio" by Rush.

TRACK 141

Here's an example in a minor key. The progression is a simple i–VII–III–VI in A minor, but we've applied a few first-inversion chords. The first time through the progression, instead of jumping up to the note C, we've inverted the III chord to a C/E, which puts the 3rd of the chord in the bass as a nice leading tone into the VI chord, F. The second time through the progression, we've inverted the VII chord to G/B, which creates a nice melodic line into the root-position C chord.

TRACK 142

It's definitely helpful to learn all of the arpeggios in first inversion, too, enabling you to play arpeggiated bass figures and know where the 5ths and roots are located when played above the 3rds. Here are some basic patterns for the first-inversion major and minor arpeggios. The root notes are still indicated with white dots, but the 3rd is the lowest-sounding note.

**First Inversion
C Major Arpeggio**

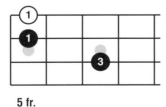

5 fr.

**First Inversion
A Minor Arpeggio**

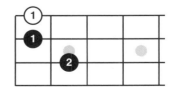

2 fr.

The following exercise covers all of the first-inversion arpeggios in the key of A major. Note the additional pattern for the 7th step, G#°/B.

TRACK 143

SECOND INVERSION

Second inversion—playing the 5th in the bass—is less common than first inversion because it doesn't create as much of a melodic effect. The reason for this is that the interval between a root note and the 5th below it is a perfect 4th, which sounds slightly more dissonant when the lowest note in the overall tonality is the bottom pitch of a perfect 4th interval. Considering the low frequencies of the bass guitar, these inversions tend to sound strange—for example, if you play a low open E under an A chord. That said, they can work in an interesting way when you use notes in the mid-level range of the instrument.

In this first example, the bass follows the root notes the first time through the progression, then uses second inversion for the chords at the end of the second round (in measure 8).

TRACK 144

This next example is reminiscent of the progression in Led Zeppelin's "Babe, I'm Gonna Leave You." It combines both first- and second-inversion chords to create a bass line that descends in steps from the tonic Am to the major dominant chord, E.

TRACK 145

Here are some basic patterns for the second-inversion major and minor arpeggios. The root notes are indicated with white dots, but the 5th is now the lowest-sounding note.

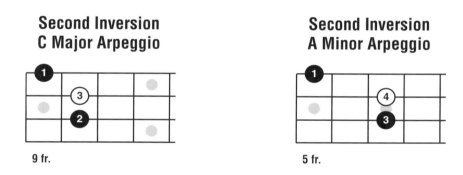

The following exercise covers all of the second-inversion arpeggios in the key of F major. Note the additional pattern for the 7th step, E°/B♭.

TRACK 146

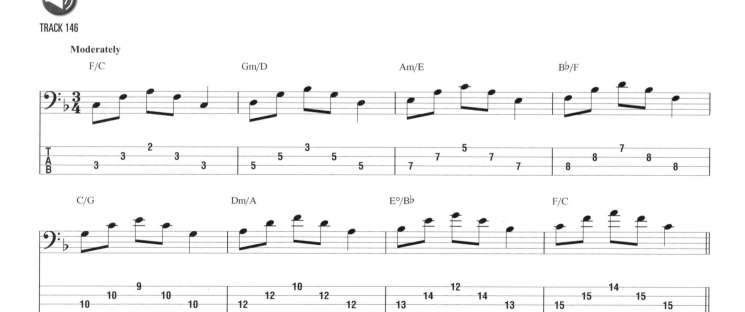

OTHER USEFUL INVERSIONS

Although the use of first or second inversion is more popular in constructing bass lines, there are some other interesting inversions bass players can use to alter the tonal landscape. Let's take a look at a few ideas that work.

Third Inversion

If first inversion involves playing the 3rd in the bass, and second inversion involves playing the 5th in the bass, it logically follows that *third inversion* involves playing the 7th in the bass since it's the next chord tone in the sequence. Oftentimes you'll see this used as part of a descending melodic line in a minor key, to connect the tonic to the VI chord. You can also use it to connect to a first-inversion major IV chord on your way to the VI chord. Both examples are shown below in the key of A minor.

TRACK 147

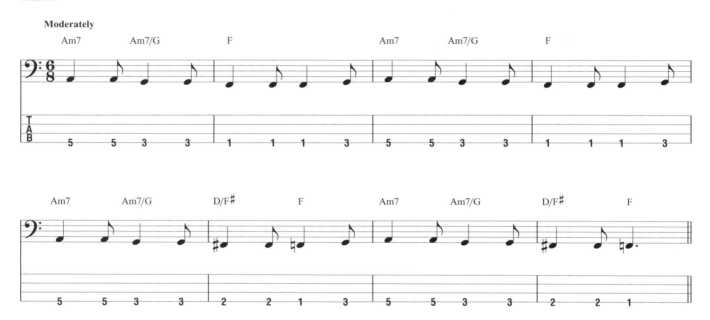

The progression above starts with Am7 in root position, then halfway through the measure, the bass plays the minor 7th, G, which leads nicely to the root-position F chord. In the second line of music, we've inserted the first-inversion IV chord, D/F♯, which connects chromatically to the F chord. Both examples work. It should be noted that the guitar or keyboard doesn't even need to be playing the full minor seventh chord in the first measure; it still works even if they're playing a plain old Am chord. The bass sort of implies the 7th when it goes to the G; however, this might not need to be called Am7/G in that case. If it really doesn't sound like a clear minor seventh chord, you might see it analyzed as just Am/G, which accounts for the bass note without needing to pigeonhole the chord as a true minor seventh. This is because the note is being played so far below the tonic in the tonal landscape.

Another point should be made here regarding third-inversion major seventh chords: they don't usually sound so good! In most cases, if you try playing the major 7th in the bass to force an inversion, since the note is a half step away from the tonic in a much lower octave, it's probably just going to sound like you hit a wrong note—you'll sound like you meant to play the root and landed a half step flat. The clash in frequencies is usually just too much. The reason the minor 7th works is because it's a whole step away from the tonic. Couple that with the fact that the other instruments are an octave higher—at least—and the interval between the bass and the guitar or keyboard will sound a lot like a 9th, which is perfectly acceptable, tonally.

Playing the 6th in the Bass

Here's where you can really apply the power of the bass and earn your paycheck. This cool maneuver will allow you to completely change the chord and its function all on your own. Let's first take a look at a simple, unaltered i–VII–VI–VII progression in A minor, with the bass playing the root notes.

TRACK 148

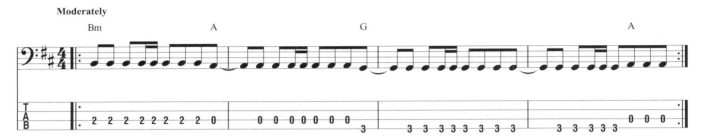

Now, without changing the guitar progression or backing track at all, let's change some of the bass notes to the 6th on a few of the chords, indicated by slash chord symbols in the analysis. Play through the example and then we'll break it down theoretically.

TRACK 149

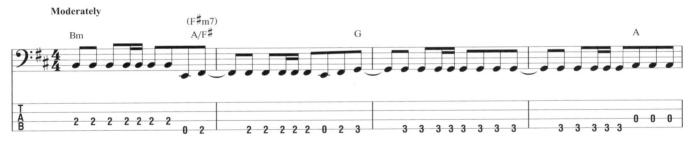

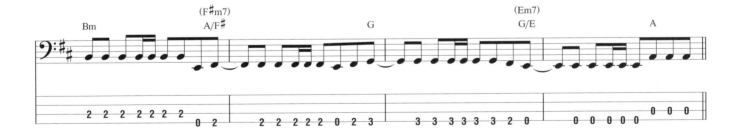

You'll remember from relative major/minor theory that the 6th transposed down an octave is actually a 3rd below the root note. Without affecting the notes the guitar is playing, the bass has actually invented an entire new root note below the guitar part. For example, the A triad consists of the R–3–5 (A–C♯–E), but the bass is now playing a low 6th (F♯) below the chord, forcing the perception that the guitar is now playing the ♭3–5–♭7 of the chord (F♯m7) instead, with the bass playing the new implied root (F♯) on its own. *Violà!* The second time through the progression, we pull the same trick with the G chord in the last measure by playing the 6th (E) in the bass. This creates an implied Em7 chord. We've indicated the implied chords in parentheses above the chord symbols for reference, but you'll almost always see them written simply as A/F♯ or G/E.

We're not done yet. We just saw how adding the major 6th below a major triad will create a new minor seventh chord. Mathematically, the rules of music theory dictate that you can create a similar effect with minor triads. By adding the *minor* 6th below a *minor* triad, you'll create a new, implied *major seventh* chord. Consider the Am chord, containing the notes A–C–E. The minor 6th in A minor is the note F, and when played by the bass, the result is an overall tonality consisting of F–A–C–E: an Fmaj7 chord. Let's combine this new inversion with some of the other inversions for our next example. In the first half, the bass plays root notes against the simple guitar progression; in the second half, we manipulate the line, incorporating multiple inversions to create our melody. As before, the implied chords are indicated in parentheses above the standard chord symbols.

TRACK 150

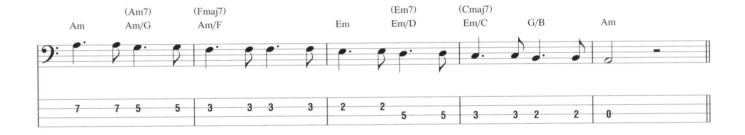

QUICK REVIEW:

- Root position occurs when the root note is the lowest-sounding note in the chord.
- First inversion occurs when the 3rd is the lowest-sounding note in the chord.
- Second inversion occurs when the 5th is the lowest-sounding note in the chord.
- Third inversion occurs when the 7th is the lowest-sounding note in the chord.
- By playing the major 6th below a major triad, the bass can imply a minor seventh chord, with the bass note functioning as the implied root note.
- By playing the minor 6th below a minor triad, the bass can imply a major seventh chord, with the bass note functioning as the implied root note.

Chapter 12: Non-Chord Tones

Non-chord tones refer to notes that do not specifically belong to the chord or arpeggio being played. These notes are especially popular with bass players when constructing melodic lines; they can refer to other scale tones outside the chord, or even chromatic notes that are outside the key. There are several different types of non-chord tones. In this chapter, we'll explore the most common ways they're used by bass players.

PASSING TONES

Passing tones are notes that fall between the notes of an arpeggio, used to melodically pass from one chord tone to the next. They can also be used to connect from the root note of one chord to the root note of the next chord in a progression. We've already seen examples of this in previous chapters, most notably with the chromatic passing tone in the blues scale, but let's examine the different types of passing tones in more detail now. There are two basic types of passing tones: *diatonic*—scale tones that already exist in the key, and *chromatic*—notes outside the key that connect from one chord or scale tone to the next in half-step increments.

This first example demonstrates how you can use chromatic passing tones to connect the root notes in a simple power-chord progression. The first two measures feature just the root notes, then the bass line is repeated, with the chromatic passing tones added in the third and fourth measures.

TRACK 151

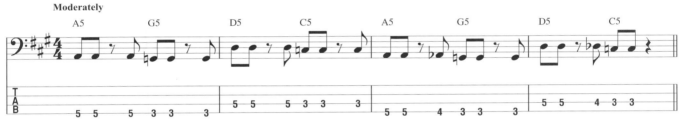

This next example, in the key of B minor, uses the notes of the minor scale as diatonic passing tones to connect from chord to chord in a i–III–VII–VI progression. The first four measures are pretty straightforward. When the progression repeats, there are a few more interesting passages. On the D chord, the D major arpeggio is outlined, but on beat 4, the note G is used as a diatonic passing tone to connect to the root note of the next chord, A. On beat 3 of the following measure, the bass drops down to the 5th of the A chord (E), and then uses the note F♯ as a diatonic passing tone to the root of the next chord, G.

TRACK 152

119

In the following example, the arpeggios in a ♭VII–IV–I progression are outlined, but they also incorporate the perfect 4th above each chord to move diatonically from the 3rd to the 5th. This makes the bass line more melodic. When the progression gets to the tonic, E, in measure 3, the bass continues to climb up the scale but flats the 7th to a D♮, giving the chord a dominant feel. You're welcome to try the major 7th, D♯, at the sixth fret instead so you can hear the difference.

TRACK 153

This next example expands on the previous idea and combines diatonic and chromatic passing tones, creating full chromatic passages between the chord tones. The progression is a simple I–V in D major. It starts on the tonic, D, then drops down to the 3rd of the D chord, F♯, and climbs chromatically to the tonic of the V chord, A (which, coincidentally, is the 5th of the D chord as well). On the A chord, the line jumps to the 2nd, a diatonic passing tone, and climbs chromatically from there to the I chord again.

TRACK 154

NEIGHBOR TONES

Neighbor tones are non-chord tones that are a half or whole step away from a chord tone in either direction. Neighbor tones are approached from the chord tone adjacent to them, and then return back to the same chord tone. The following example contains a neighbor tone a whole step below the octave during the Am chord. For the Em chord, neighbor tones above and below the octave are used.

TRACK 155

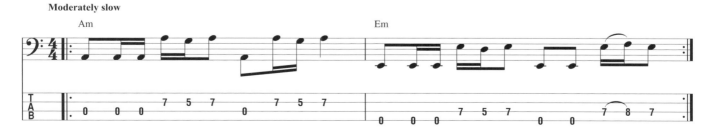

For this next example, let's revisit our classic rock 'n' roll bass line that outlines the major arpeggios. The 6th is added as a neighbor tone from the 5th of the chord to make the line a little more melodically interesting.

TRACK 156

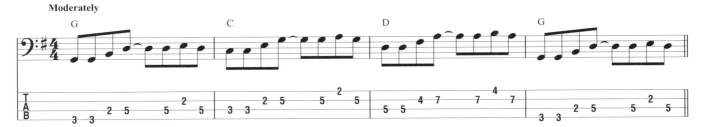

Here's one more popular way of using neighbor tones. Bass players are fond of approaching root notes from a whole step away by using grace notes or hammer-ons. This groove in A minor uses the G a whole step below the tonic as a neighbor tone.

TRACK 157

APPOGGIATURAS

An *appoggiatura* is a non-chord tone that is approached by a leap (an interval wider than a step), but resolves to a chord tone a step away. Here's an example of a rock bass line that contains a few simple appoggiaturas placed either above or below the resolution.

TRACK 158

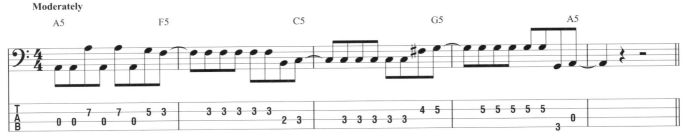

Appoggiaturas don't always have to happen when the harmony changes. Let's take a look at a variation of the classic rock line from the previous page. Here, the 6th is approached from a leap and then resolves to the 5th, making it an appoggiatura instead of a neighbor tone.

TRACK 159

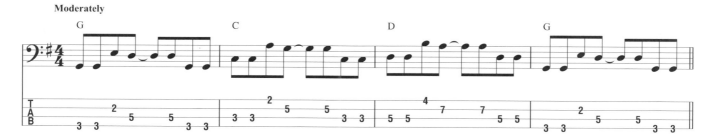

Appoggiaturas are also popular in walking bass lines when used with chromatic resolution to the next chord's root note from a half step away. Here's a simple example using a ii–V–I–V progression. Notice that the last note of the second measure (F#) functions as an appoggiatura, but it's also the 3rd of the V chord, as well as the leading tone in the key.

TRACK 160

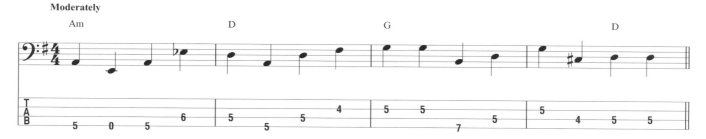

SUSPENSIONS

The most popular *suspensions* are the suspended 4th (sus4) and suspended 2nd (sus2) chords. A suspension occurs when the 3rd of the chord is replaced with the 2nd or the 4th. These chords have a strong desire and tendency to resolve back to their regular R–3–5 states, but it's not always necessary, particularly in the case of the sus2 chord, which often functions just fine without resolution. Although minor-chord suspensions are not unheard of, major-chord suspensions are much more commonplace. Listen to the following guitar track to hear some of the popular suspensions and resolutions guitarists often apply to open-position chords.

TRACK 161

D Dsus4 D |D Dsus2 D |C Csus4 C |C Csus2 C |

A Asus4 A |A Asus2 A ||

It's not really recommended that bass players hang on the suspended notes while they occur, unless they're part of a melodic figure. Because of the low frequency of the bass notes, playing 2nds or 4ths will obscure the suspensions in the guitar or keyboard and make the chords sound more like odd inversions. There are exceptions, like when you're playing a solo high up on the fretboard or playing a melodic theme. Also, in the instance of a suspended 2nd, you can get away with playing 2nds above the octave since these will sound a lot like 9ths and blend nicely with the chords. For the most part, however, you need to know where the suspensions are located so you know what notes *not* to play. Suspended chords contain no 3rds, so it's essential that you're not playing major 3rds or regular R–3–5 triads when one is occurring in the progression. Be aware of where they are located and let the music breathe so that the suspensions and resolutions played by the other instruments have the desired effect. Once the suspension resolves, 3rds sound fine; you may even try to emphasize the resolution itself, but make sure you're doing it in time with the progression. Here's an example of a melodic bass line in the upper register that coincides with sus4 chords.

TRACK 162

This next example uses some sus2 chords that do not resolve at all. They have a fuller, more spacious sound than regular power chords. Although it's not unheard of for the bass to play a few 3rds here and there against the sus2 chords, it does dampen their effect. The point of the standalone sus2 chord is to be ambiguous—it's neither major nor minor in nature. On a side note, if the 2nd and 3rd are both present in the chord, it is referred to as an "add2 chord" instead. Your best choices when playing against a sus2 chord are to stick to roots, 5ths, and octaves, with some 9ths (2nds) thrown in for melody. You can also use the 6th from the major pentatonic scale effectively, as shown below.

TRACK 163

PEDAL TONES

As it applies in rock and pop music, a *pedal tone* is a note that is sustained or played continuously in the bass while the chords played by the guitar and keyboard change above it. This was extremely popular in late-'80s hair-band music, when it was common for bass players to thump away eighth notes on a single low note for most of a song. Although not very exciting for the bass player, it had the desired effect of creating a big, loud, thunderous rhythm section that would become a signature element of the arena-rock sound.

The following example in E minor relegates the bass player to straight quarter notes on the open fourth string while the guitar plays a chordal riff above it.

TRACK 164

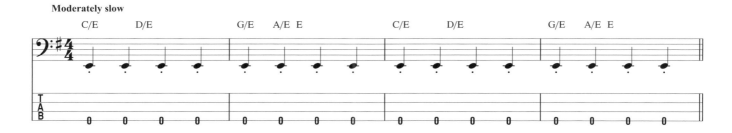

Here's an example that's similar to "You've Got Another Thing Comin'" by Judas Priest. In this one, the bass joins up with the guitar at the end of the progression to play the riff together.

TRACK 165

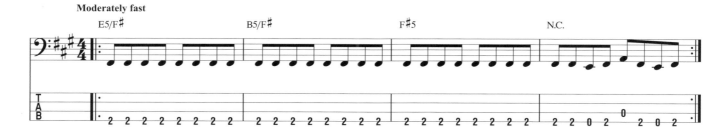

CHORD EXTENSIONS

As we discussed in the chapter on intervals, the process of stacking 3rds to produce triads and seventh chords can be continued up past the octave to yield ninth, 11th, and 13th chords. For jazz guitarists, this is an extensive study and a great deal of it doesn't concern the average bass player. We've already discussed major 9ths, which are the same as the 2nd but an octave higher. Beyond that, bass players generally focus on the popular chord tones—the root, 3rd, 5th, and 7th—and leave the heavy soloing theory to the jazz guitarist. You may encounter chord names that contain extensive variations and combinations of the upper chord tones from time to time—♭9, #9, #11—but as a bass player, you won't really be playing these notes in the lower register anyway. If you'd like to familiarize yourself with these intervals more, practice stacking 3rds and naming the notes. There are numerous chord books that you can pick up and dissect in order to map out the arpeggios on the bass more thoroughly.

Analyzing Non-Chord Tones

As we've seen, there are often different ways to analyze a piece of music, and it often depends on the function of the notes. Most of the time, the simplest solution is the best one. You could analyze notes in so much detail that you lose the point of the process—which is to give you a framework and a way of thinking so you can apply these discoveries to your own playing. You can pick apart non-chord tones forever and claim that each one is actually a 9th, or a 13th, or a #11th, but usually they're just passing tones, neighbor tones, or chromatic passages. A minor 3rd played an octave higher could be considered a minor 10th, or it could even be considered a #9, but does that information help you determine your note choices? Or is it just bogging you down? Once you have a firm grasp of the material in this book, if you choose to pursue complex jazz or classical studies, you may find yourself in those waters. Ultimately, you'll have to decide for yourself how far down the rabbit hole you want to go.

QUICK REVIEW:

- Passing tones are approached by a step and left by a step in the same direction.

- Neighbor tones are approached by a step (from a chord tone) and left by a step in the opposite direction (back to the original chord tone).

- Appoggiaturas are approached by a leap and left by a step (to a chord tone).

- The two common suspensions are the sus2 and the sus4, which are used as substitutions for the 3rd.

- A pedal tone is a note sustained or played continuously while the chords change above it.

- The process of stacking 3rds to produce triads and seventh chords can be continued up past the octave to yield ninth, 11th, and 13th chords. Jazz chords contain many variations and combinations of these chord extensions.

Chapter 13: The Modes

A *mode* is an inversion of a scale. The most common modes are the scales that are built on the individual steps of the major scale. There are seven different notes in a major scale; therefore, there are seven modes—one for each step of the scale.

MODAL THEORY

Let's start by briefly exploring the modes and the theory behind them, using the notes in the key of C. Since the C major scale contains only natural notes (no sharps or flats), all of the modes derived from the key of C will also contain only natural notes. The first mode is the *Ionian* mode, and it uses the note C as the tonic; therefore, the Ionian mode is exactly the same as the major scale (Ionian is just the modal name for the major scale).

TRACK 166

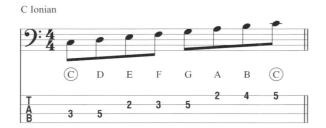

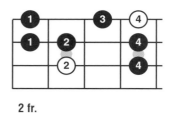

If we play from D to the octave D using all of the notes in the C major scale, this gives us our second mode: *Dorian*. We're still using all of the same notes as the key of C major, but now we're considering D to be the tonic instead of C. This yields an entirely new series of half steps and whole steps. Now the half steps occur between the 2nd and 3rd, and between the 6th and 7th.

Just as with the relative major and minor scales, it can be said that D Dorian is the relative Dorian mode to C major (Ionian) since they both contain all of the same notes. Utilizing the natural notes from D to D, the following scale diagram, notation, and tab show one octave of the D Dorian mode. Since D is now considered the root note, the Ds are indicated with white circles in the scale diagram.

TRACK 167

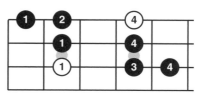

126

Using this same method, we can continue to build a new mode on every step of the C major scale, each with its own unique series of half steps and whole steps. The remaining modes, in order, are *Phrygian*, *Lydian*, *Mixolydian*, *Aeolian*, and *Locrian*. The chart below shows each mode's formula of half steps and whole steps. Following the chart, we'll continue to show one octave of each of the remaining modes by using scale diagrams, notation, and tab.

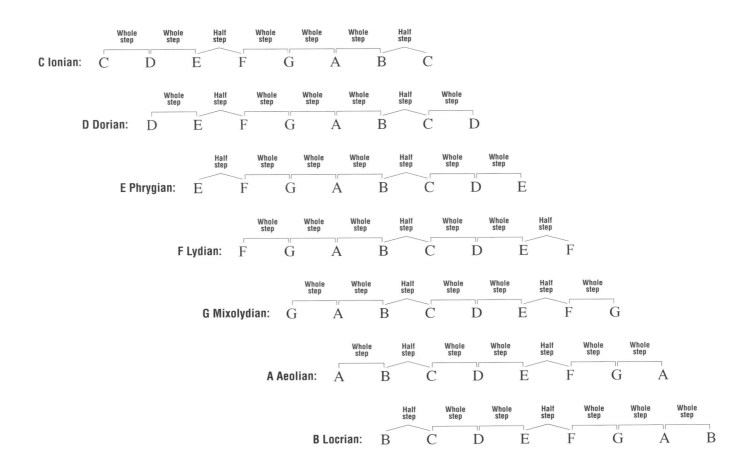

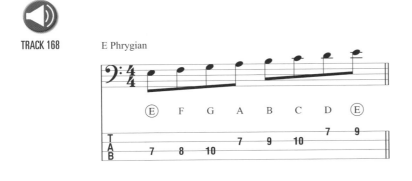

TRACK 168   E Phrygian

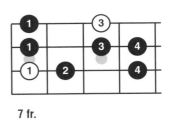

7 fr.

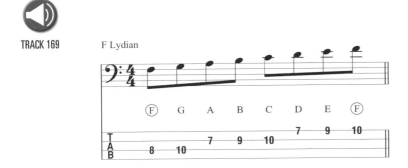

TRACK 169   F Lydian

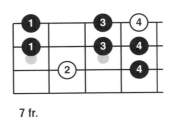

7 fr.

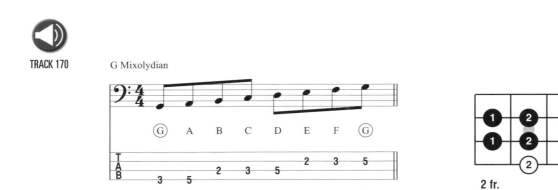

TRACK 170   G Mixolydian

The mode built on the 6th step of the major scale is the *Aeolian* mode, which is exactly the same as the natural minor scale; Aeolian is just the modal name for the natural minor scale.

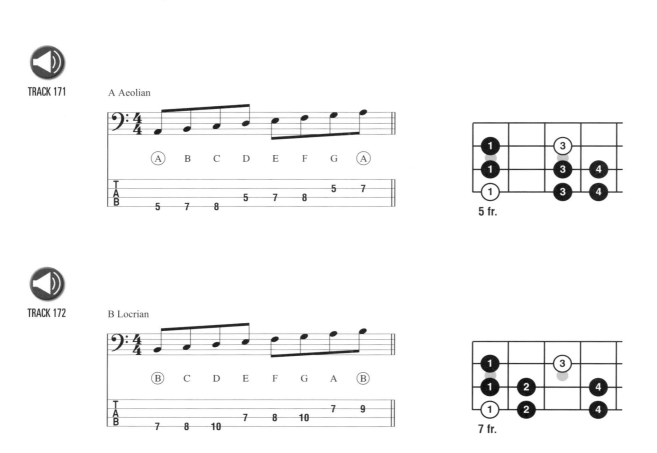

TRACK 171   A Aeolian

TRACK 172   B Locrian

Now that you've learned where these modal scales come from, let's examine some ways in which they can be used. Beginner students of the modes are often confused by their application, and sometimes they don't see the point in them at all. You might assume that, like the arpeggios, you can apply a different modal scale to each chord in a progression. For example, say you're playing a song in the key of C major. When you're on the ii chord (Dm), you can play a D Dorian scale, or when you're on the V chord (G), you can play a G Mixolydian scale. This may be true in theory; however, it doesn't produce much of an effect since you're still only using notes in the key of C major and trying to shift the emphasis to the root note of each individual chord. It seems like an awful lot of information to have swimming around in your head when all you really need to do is play in the key of C and keep track of the chord progression. For this reason, many students don't understand the usefulness of the scales once they learn them. The next section lends a different perspective.

Major-Sounding Modes

Modal key signatures aren't used very often in popular music. If a passage of music utilizes D Dorian, you probably won't see it presented in written form with no sharps or flats in the key signature, even though there are no sharps or flats in the scale. Instead, you'll almost always encounter music written in traditional major or minor keys. If we compare the different modal scales, we'll have a better understanding of how they can be applied in regular major and minor keys. The basic tonality of a scale—whether it's generally a major- or minor-sounding scale—is determined by the 3rd of the scale. The Ionian, Lydian, and Mixolydian scales all contain major 3rds, while the rest of the modes contain minor 3rds. Therefore, we can say that Ionian, Lydian, and Mixolydian are all (more or less) *major-sounding* modes.

Let's compare the Ionian scale with the Lydian and Mixolydian modes transposed so that C is the root note (tonic) of each scale. Notice how similar the C Lydian and C Mixolydian scales are to the C Ionian (major) scale—only one note in each scale differs from the major scale. The Lydian mode contains a sharped 4th, while the Mixolydian mode contains a flatted 7th. Getting to know these basic similarities between the scales will help you to demystify and recognize the modes, and give you some ideas on how to substitute them when you're playing in major and minor keys. If you've already perfected your major and minor scales, knowing these slight differences will make it much easier to memorize and master the rest of the modes.

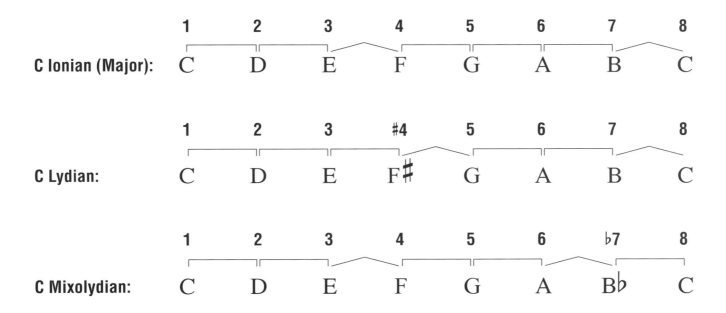

Let's reinforce this concept by examining the C Lydian and C Mixolydian modes in notation and tab, both starting on the third string at the third fret, so that you can compare them directly to the C major scale shown at the beginning of the chapter. In the accompanying scale diagrams, the #4th of the Lydian mode and the ♭7th of the Mixolydian mode are indicated with gray circles.

TRACK 173   C Lydian

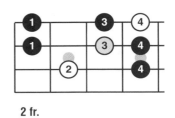

129

C Mixolydian

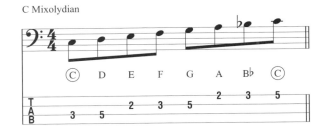

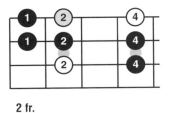

2 fr.

Minor-Sounding Modes

The Dorian, Phrygian, Aeolian, and Locrian modes all contain minor 3rds; therefore, we can say they are all (more or less) *minor-sounding* modes. Since the A Aeolian mode and the A minor scale are the same and contain only natural notes, let's compare the Aeolian mode with the Dorian, Phrygian, and Locrian modes transposed so that A is the root note (tonic) of each scale. The Dorian and Phrygian modes differ from the Aeolian mode by only one note: Dorian contains a major 6th, while Phrygian contains a minor 2nd. The Locrian mode differs from Aeolian by two notes: a minor 2nd and a flatted (diminished) 5th.

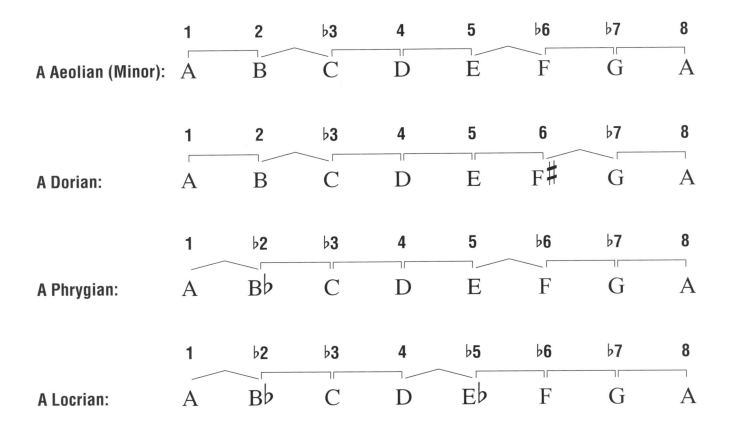

Now let's take a look at the A Dorian, A Phrygian, and A Locrian modes in notation and tab on the following page, all starting on the fourth string at the fifth fret, to give you an easy comparison to the A Aeolian (minor) mode. The notes that differ from the Aeolian (minor) mode are indicated with gray circles.

TRACK 175   A Dorian

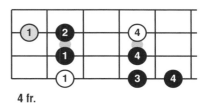

4 fr.

TRACK 176   A Phrygian

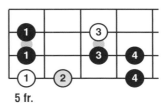

5 fr.

TRACK 177   A Locrian

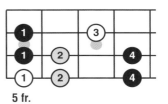

5 fr.

Memorizing the Modes

The scale comparisons really come in handy as shortcuts to memorizing the modes. At this point, you should know your major (Ionian) and minor (Aeolian) scales cold and be able to play them in any position on the fretboard. Rather than learn all of the positions of the remaining five modes individually, use the knowledge presented above to alter the major and minor scales by one or two notes to play the modes. Playing the Mixolydian and Phrygian modes should be especially easy. Simply flat the 7th (the note below the tonic) of the major scale to play Mixolydian. For Phrygian, flat the 2nd (the note above the tonic) of the minor scale. If you can keep track of where the ♭6th of the minor scale is located, raise it by a half step to play in Dorian. Remembering these shortcuts not only gives you an easier way to play the modes, but also helps you to visualize them in comparison to the major and minor scales on the fretboard, which will come in handy when you apply the scales in the coming section.

MODAL APPLICATIONS

The most effective way to apply the modes when creating bass lines or improvising is to use the modal scales as slight alterations to the regular major or minor scales, as discussed in the previous section. Although you can use any of the modes to solo, a few of them lend themselves to regular playing more than others. We'll examine some of the more popular modal applications in this section.

Mixolydian Bass Lines

The Mixolydian mode is extremely popular with bass players; it's probably used more often than the regular major scale. This is due to the flatted 7th, which presents a bluesier, dominant alteration to the major scale. Since the 7th degree is the only note that differs from the standard major scale, Mixolydian is an easy substitution when playing in a major key. In written music, you can identify the use of the Mixolydian mode by the accidentals present. For example, if a piece of music is in A major (three sharps) and all of the Gs have naturals on them, you can see that the 7th has been lowered by a half step, indicating the use of the Mixolydian mode. The following Mixolydian riff is reminiscent of Aerosmith's "Sweet Emotion" and uses many of the notes of the scale to create a melodic bass riff.

TRACK 178

Here's a I–IV progression in D major that uses the D Mixolydian mode for its melodies instead of the regular major scale. The key signature denotes D major by using two sharps, but the presence of the naturals on the Cs throughout indicate that the Mixolydian mode is used. John Paul Jones or Geddy Lee might use this approach when employing the Mixolydian mode in a major key.

TRACK 179

Dorian Bass Lines

Since the Dorian mode contains a minor 3rd, it is considered a minor-sounding mode and can be used as a substitution in minor keys. The only note that's different is the raised 6th, giving it more of a moderate sound than the full natural minor scale. Dorian isn't quite as popular as Mixolydian, but you'll still hear it used fairly often by bass players. Another observation of note is how similar the Dorian scale is to the Mixolydian scale. If you compare the two scales, their intervallic formulas are identical except for the 3rd; Mixolydian contains a major 3rd, while Dorian contains a minor 3rd. Therefore, Dorian can also be thought of as a minor-sounding version of the Mixolydian mode. Here are a couple of bass lines using the A Dorian mode, notated in the standard A minor key signature.

TRACK 180

TRACK 181

Be Careful of the Chord Progression

When applying the Dorian mode in a minor key, some chords and specific progressions can be problematic. Ultimately, you'll need to stay alert and make sure the raised 6th isn't clashing. For example, in A Dorian, the 6th is the note F♯. Some of the more popular progressions in the key of A minor utilize the VI chord, which is an F major chord. Needless to say, you don't want to be caught playing F♯s against an F chord. This doesn't necessarily mean you can't use Dorian at all, but you should try to avoid using the 6th degree on that particular chord. That said, there are other chords in the key of A minor where the F♯ is preferable. For example, the ii chord in the key is a B° chord, which contains a flatted 5th (F♮). By using Dorian to raise the note to F♯, the ii chord becomes a regular minor chord. All of this theoretical information can help you to avoid pitfalls, but a good rule of thumb is to always trust your ear and take note of what works—the theory is always available to explain why.

Locrian Bass Lines

The Locrian mode is the darkest and most sinister mode. It didn't get much play until the darker heavy metal bands popularized it, mostly using it for riff-based music. It's unlikely that you'll use it for bass improvisation, but you'll encounter it in many riffs by bands like Metallica, Slayer, and Black Sabbath. Let's take a look at the E Locrian mode, shown below using the E minor key signature of one sharp, since this is usually the key in which you'll encounter the Locrian mode. Notice the presence of the natural to lower the 2nd step to F♮, and the flat to lower the 5th to B♭.

TRACK 182

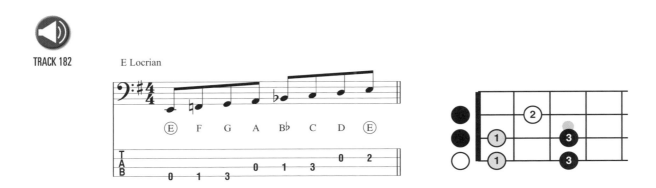

Here's a typical metal riff using the E Locrian mode in open position as shown above. Remember: in written music, E Locrian is easily identified by the presence of F♮s and B♭s in the music notation.

TRACK 183

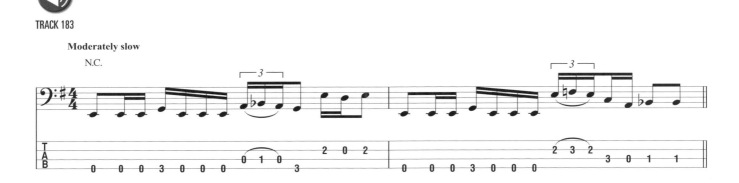

The following is an example of an E Locrian metal riff. This one still utilizes the low open E, but spreads the notes of the scale out exclusively along the fourth string, giving the riff a heavier feel.

TRACK 184

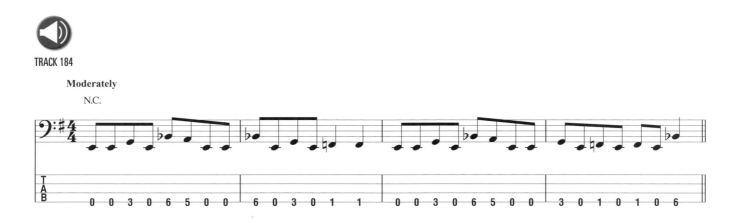

134

QUICK REVIEW:

- Here are the names of the seven modes, in order, followed by their unique intervallic formulas:

  1. **Ionian:** W–W–H–W–W–W–H
  2. **Dorian:** W–H–W–W–W–H–W
  3. **Phrygian:** H–W–W–W–H–W–W
  4. **Lydian:** W–W–W–H–W–W–H
  5. **Mixolydian:** W–W–H–W–W–H–W
  6. **Aeolian:** W–H–W–W–H–W–W
  7. **Locrian:** H–W–W–H–W–W–W

- Ionian, Lydian, and Mixolydian are major-sounding modes because they contain major 3rds.

- Dorian, Phrygian, Aeolian, and Locrian are minor-sounding modes because they contain minor 3rds.

REVIEW QUIZ

Add the necessary accidentals to complete the proper spelling for each of the following modes. To determine the accidentals, you can either use each mode's intervallic formula, or you can determine the mode's relative major key in order to figure out what the key signature is. The answer key is at the bottom of the following page.

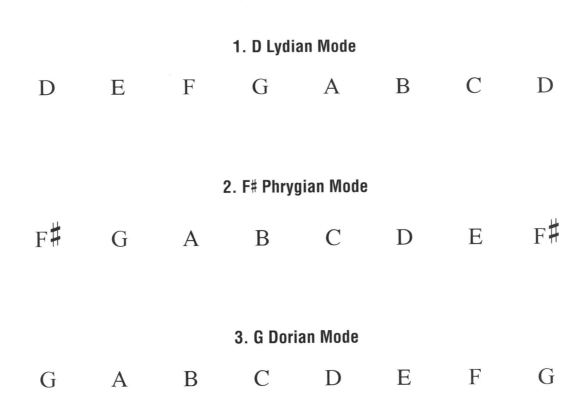

1. D Lydian Mode

D   E   F   G   A   B   C   D

2. F♯ Phrygian Mode

F♯   G   A   B   C   D   E   F♯

3. G Dorian Mode

G   A   B   C   D   E   F   G

4. B Mixolydian Mode

B   C   D   E   F   G   A   B

5. B♭ Aeolian Mode

B♭   C   D   E   F   G   A   B♭

6. G Locrian Mode

G   A   B   C   D   E   F   G

7. E Dorian Mode

E   F   G   A   B   C   D   E

8. D♭ Mixolydian Mode

D♭   E   F   G   A   B   C   D♭

Chapter 14: Advanced Scales

We've already covered most of the scales that you'll use as a bass player, but to be thorough, let's explore some additional scales you may encounter in jazz and other progressive genres. We'll start out with a few essential variations of the minor scale that get frequent use, then finish up with some other complex scales. Some of these scales are more commonly used by jazz guitarists for soloing, but they're worth briefly exploring here.

THE HARMONIC MINOR SCALE

The *harmonic minor scale* is a variation of the natural minor scale, containing a raised (major) 7th in place of the traditional minor 7th. This creates a unique scale that has an augmented 2nd (one-and-a-half steps) between the 6th and 7th steps of the scale. Here's one octave of the A harmonic minor scale; the raised 7th is indicated using a gray circle on the fretboard diagram.

TRACK 185

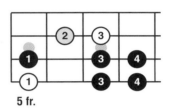

The harmonic minor scale was initially used primarily to build chords (harmonize) from the notes of the minor scale. It evolved from a necessity to have a major dominant (V) chord in the minor key, making for a stronger traditional V–i cadence. You'll remember in the earlier chapter on harmonization, in minor keys, the v chord is naturally a minor chord. The 3rd of that chord is the 7th step of the minor scale; therefore, by raising it a half step, the minor chord becomes major. The raised 3rd then produces a strong leading tone to tonic resolution within the V–i cadence.

For example, in the key of A minor (shown above), the dominant chord is built on the note E. The 7th step of the harmonic minor scale is the note G♯, which is the major 3rd of the E chord. It is also the leading tone in the key, creating the strong G♯–A resolution within the V–i cadence—the E major chord (V) to the A minor chord (i).

While the harmonic minor scale evolved as a basis for chords, it has also been used melodically due to its unique augmented 2nd interval between the 6th and 7th steps. It's very popular in Middle Eastern music, and is used extensively in heavy metal, progressive rock, and neo-classical genres, especially by guitar players.

Harmonizing the Harmonic Minor Scale

Analyzing a strict, full harmonization of the harmonic minor scale yields some unique and interesting results. While is does manage to achieve the desired major V chord, it also creates a few other chords that can either be exciting or problematic, depending on the genre and application. Here's a full harmonization of the A harmonic minor scale. Notice that it's still written in the key of A minor, with the necessary G♯s added to the notation.

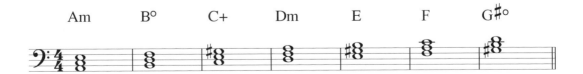

The three chords that are affected by the scale's raised 7th are the mediant, dominant, and leading tone, as you can see in the notation on the previous page (the chords containing G#s). Here's a chart with the chord names, Roman-numeral analysis, and the chord types indicated below.

i	ii°	III+	iv	V	VI	vii°
Am	**B°**	**C+**	**Dm**	**E**	**F**	**G#°**
minor	diminished	augmented	minor	major	major	diminished

By raising the 7th of the scale, we've achieved the desired dominant V chord, and we've also got a diminished vii chord, just like there is in the major keys. Notice that the root note of the vii chord is the altered note, so there is a G#° chord now instead of a G chord. The most interesting chord is the III+ chord. This is the first time we've encountered an augmented chord that occurs in a scale harmonization. It's used infrequently, but it did start to gain popularity in the late classical period around the time of Beethoven.

Here's an arpeggio exercise for bass that utilizes all of the triads built on the A harmonic minor scale. This will help you remember the order of the chords and hear their unique qualities.

TRACK 186

The preceding information represents a full harmonization of the harmonic minor scale; however, you probably won't encounter popular music today that strictly adheres to these chords throughout an entire piece or progression. It's much more likely that you'll find music written mostly in the natural minor key that occasionally borrows the raised 7th just to alter the dominant chord. The following familiar E minor progression is a good example. Notice that the VII chord (D) is a major chord built on the ♭7th from the natural minor scale, but the V chord (B) uses the raised 7th in order to achieve the major dominant chord.

TRACK 187

Here's an example that cycles through most of the chords in the key of D minor. The last chord (A) is the major V chord, borrowing the raised 7th from the harmonic minor scale. All of the other chords are derived from the natural minor scale harmonization.

TRACK 188

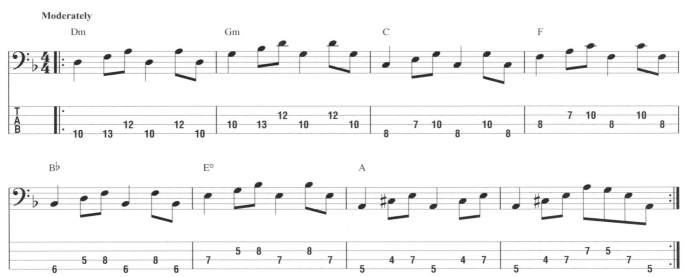

To be thorough, let's go ahead and extend the harmonization of the harmonic minor scale to add the 7th to each chord. It's unlikely you'll encounter some of these chords in popular music, such as the m(maj7) or the fully °7th, but they're worth taking note of to complete this theoretical study.

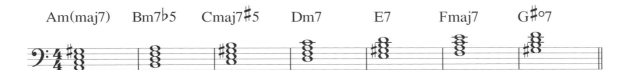

The following arpeggio exercise utilizes all of the seventh chords built on the A harmonic minor scale.

TRACK 189

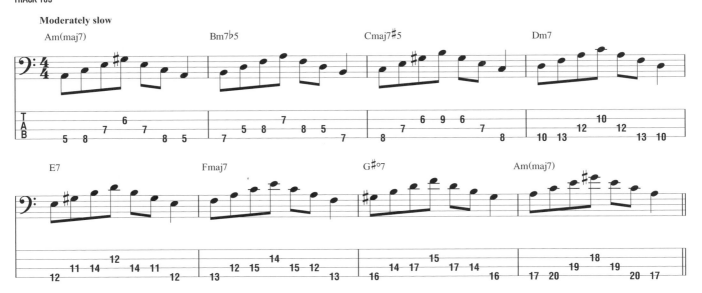

THE MELODIC MINOR SCALE

The ascending *melodic minor scale* contains a major 6th and a major 7th. The descending form is the same as the natural minor scale. Traditionally, this is how the scale was used in classical music, but in jazz applications it's common to use the major 6th and 7th both ascending and descending (often referred to as the *jazz melodic minor scale*). Here's one octave of the A melodic minor scale; the raised 6th and 7th are indicated with gray circles. The fretboard diagram shows a suggested fingering that includes a position-shift pivot with the fourth finger.

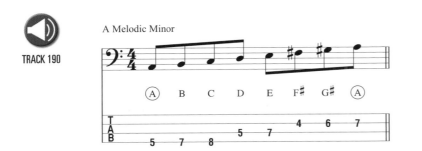

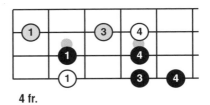

A Melodic Minor

TRACK 190

4 fr.

Melodic minor is used for playing melody or soloing (hence the *melodic* minor name), so there's no need to harmonize the scale. On bass, it can sometimes be substituted during the popular ii–V–i cadence.

The following chart compares the three different forms of the minor scale in the key of A minor.

	1	2	b3	4	5	b6	b7	8
A Natural Minor:	A	B	C	D	E	F	G	A

	1	2	b3	4	5	b6	7	8
A Harmonic Minor:	A	B	C	D	E	F	G♯	A

	1	2	b3	4	5	6	7	8
A Melodic Minor:	A	B	C	D	E	F♯	G♯	A

Another observation that can be made about the melodic minor scale is how closely related it is to the major scale. The only difference is the 3rd: in the major scale, it's a major 3rd; in the melodic minor, it's a minor 3rd, which makes it one of the minor-sounding scales even though the rest of the scale is identical to major. It's much easier to visualize the major scale across the fretboard and then just flat the 3rd, than it is to try to remember where all of the 6ths and 7ths are located. The following chart compares the melodic minor scale to its parallel major scale.

	1	2	b3	4	5	6	7	8
A Melodic Minor:	A	B	C	D	E	F♯	G♯	A

	1	2	3	4	5	6	7	8
A Major:	A	B	C♯	D	E	F♯	G♯	A

To reinforce this concept, here are a few more fingerings for the A melodic minor scale that closely resemble the familiar major scale fingerings you already know. The minor 3rd is represented by a gray dot.

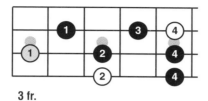

3 fr.

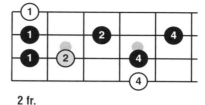

2 fr.

MORE COMPLEX SCALES

The following scales can also be used for soloing or creating riffs. Some are based on the diatonic scales we've explored so far, while some are simply a series of intervals. These advanced scales aren't used by bass players as often as guitar players, but there are numerous jazz studies outside the scope of this book that you can explore if you'd like to study these scales further.

Whole Tone Scale

The *whole tone scale* is made up of a symmetrical series of whole steps; the scale contains no half-step intervals. Because of this, any note can act as the root note and the intervallic formula remains the same. The scale is shown below, starting on the note C.

TRACK 191

C Whole Tone

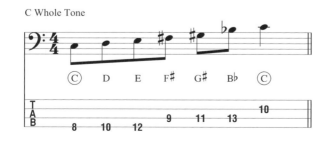

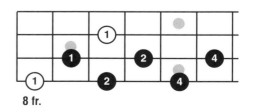

8 fr.

Diminished Scales

A *diminished scale* is a symmetrical scale made up of alternating half and whole steps. There are two different diminished scales: the *fully diminished scale*, which begins with a whole step, and the *dominant diminished scale*, which begins with a half step. Both scales contain eight different notes.

Here's one octave of the fully diminished (whole-half) scale, beginning on the note C. This scale is generally used to solo over diminished seventh (°7) chords, which we saw earlier in this chapter while harmonizing the harmonic minor scale.

TRACK 192

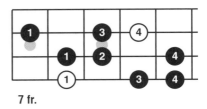

Here's one octave of the dominant diminished (half-whole) scale, which gets its name because it's often used to solo over dominant seventh chords.

TRACK 193

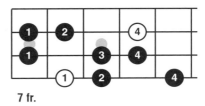

The Altered Scale

The *altered scale* is somewhat similar in intervals to the dominant diminished scale, but the altered scale contains seven notes instead of eight. The scale gets its name from having every interval altered except the core elements of the dominant chord: the root, 3rd, and b7th. The true spelling for the scale is R–b9–#9–3–#11–#5–b7, but it is actually enharmonic to the seventh mode of the melodic minor scale. The altered scale is sometimes referred to as the *super Locrian scale*, or the *diminished whole-tone scale*.

TRACK 194

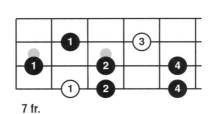

The Phrygian Dominant Scale

The *Phrygian dominant scale* is the fifth mode of the harmonic minor scale. It's often used in Indian, Middle Eastern, and flamenco music, but it can be heard in progressive metal and neo-classical as well. The scale formula for the Phrygian dominant is R–♭2–3–4–5–♭6–♭7.

TRACK 195

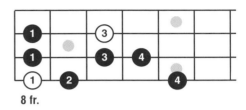

The Lydian Dominant Scale

The *Lydian dominant scale* is actually the fourth mode of the melodic minor scale. Lydian implies the ♯4th, and dominant implies the ♭7th, so the Lydian dominant contains both. It can be thought of as the Lydian mode with a ♭7th, or the Mixolydian mode with a ♯4th. It can also be thought of as a major scale with a ♯4th and a ♭7th.

TRACK 196

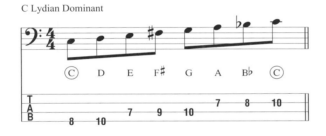

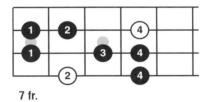

Chapter 15: Stylistic Bass Lines

Let's tie all of the elements of music theory together to explore and analyze the bass styles of some of the great rock masters and other popular players of today. The theoretical knowledge presented throughout this book can be used to dissect the bass lines of your favorite players and give you the tools you'll need to emulate them and construct your own unique bass parts.

DUFF MCKAGAN

Duff McKagan, bassist for Guns N' Roses, has a pretty straight-ahead rock style and does a good job of locking in with the kick drum, while also managing to add some melody and pentatonic riffs to his bass lines.

This example is similar to the bass in "Sweet Child O' Mine." It features a pretty straightforward rock groove and a I–♭VII–IV progression with some tasteful melodic passages and chromatic passing tones. Play through the bass line a few times first; we'll break it down and analyze it below.

TRACK 197

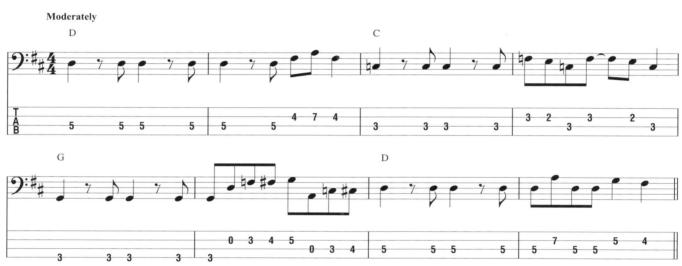

The bass starts out in the above example by laying down a solid groove on the I chord (D), and features a D major arpeggio at the end of measure 2. Moving to the ♭VII chord (C), there's a tasty melodic fill in measure 4 that features the suspended 4th resolving to the major 3rd a few times. On the IV chord (G), measure 6 has an interesting fill that uses the ♭7th and a chromatic passing tone as appoggiaturas up to the octave, then repeats this move a 4th lower to climb up towards the 5th of the G chord, which is also the tonic D. The end of the example features another suspended 4th to the major 3rd.

Duff can often be heard utilizing the blues scales, as in this next example:

TRACK 198

The previous riff features one of Duff's signature moves which involves the use of a hammer-on from the minor 3rd to the major 3rd, regardless of whether the song is in a major or minor key. This example is reminiscent of the bridge in "Mr. Brownstone." This riff style can also be heard in the bass line from "Rocket Queen."

TOM HAMILTON

Tom Hamilton of Aerosmith is one of the great unsung bass heroes to come out of the fertile rock scene of the '70s. Many rock bass players have since pointed to Hamilton as a big influence due to his excellent instincts, rock-solid groove, pocket playing, and successful songwriting.

Here's an example of a funky bass line in the style of "Walk This Way." The bass combines elements of the major and minor blues scale and the Mixolydian mode, along with tasteful chromatic passing tones. The riff at the end of the example is derived from the C blues scale. The bass slides up to the ♭7th, and includes a chromatic passing tone to the octave, but ends with the minor/major 3rds taken from the major blues scale.

TRACK 199

This next example is played with a blues shuffle and uses the notes of an E minor seventh arpeggio. In the last measure, there's a nice triplet riff on a descending E blues scale.

TRACK 200

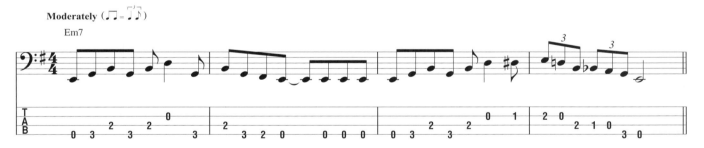

Hamilton created some great bass hooks, including quite possibly the most famous one of all time: the intro to "Sweet Emotion," the stylistic template for this next riff. The similar tone and vibe may have been inspired by Paul McCartney's great bass line in "Come Together." The riff is written in A major, but is derived from Mixolydian, indicated by the use of the ♭7th (G♮).

TRACK 201

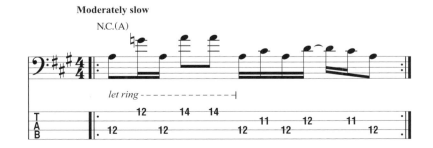

145

Aerosmith was also great at fast, heavy tracks. This next riff, similar to "Toys in the Attic," is played at a very fast tempo and takes some steady pluck-hand coordination and strength to pull it off. Notice the positioning of the scale. Instead of playing it all in open position, the meat of the riff is played up at the fifth fret. Playing at this speed in open position would make it difficult to control string noise and would surely sound sloppy. There's also a tonal benefit to the thicker-gauge third and fourth strings handling all of the notes.

TRACK 202

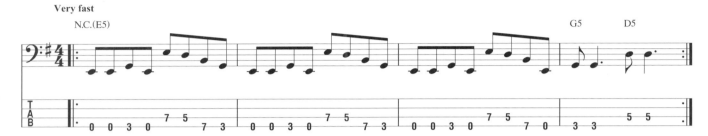

STEVE HARRIS

Iron Maiden's bass hero and principle songwriter, Steve Harris is known for his incredibly fast, strong fingerstyle technique. Although he's known for his signature gallop rhythm, he's got a few stock moves that he uses repeatedly for riffs and melodies.

Here's an example of a melodic bass line that moves with the chord changes and showcases what can be referred to as the "Steve Harris arpeggio." Instead of using major and minor 3rds, Harris instead opts for the 4th, making the arpeggiated pattern uniform throughout the progression.

TRACK 203

Similar to the 4th substitution in the previous example, Harris would sometimes use 2nds instead of minor 3rds in his minor pentatonic bass riffs. This keeps the entire riff in a uniform, 1–3–1–3 finger pattern. Although Harris is no stranger to major and minor 3rds (the main riff to "Number of the Beast" prominently features a major 3rd), he often takes the approach showcased in these two examples, creating his own unique altered scales and arpeggios. The following example of an altered pentatonic bass riff can be found in songs like "Two Minutes to Midnight."

TRACK 204

Here's another technique that Harris is fond of using during quieter instrumental sections of a song. This riff outlines the D minor scale by pivoting around the open D string and alternating the descending scale tones above it on the first string in a syncopated fashion.

TRACK 205

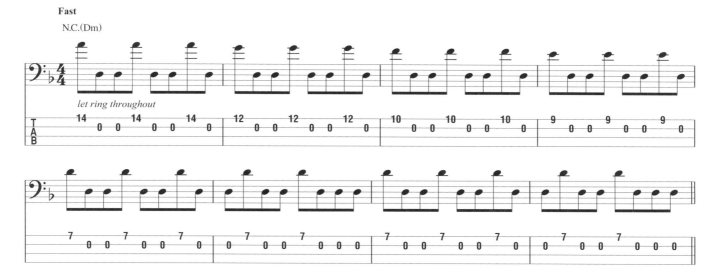

GEEZER BUTLER

Black Sabbath's Geezer Butler is a heavy metal innovator, often considered to be the godfather of metal bass. His grungy bass tone complements the Sabbath sound and has influenced metal bassists for decades. On early Black Sabbath recordings, Butler was a master of the pentatonic and blues scales, combining distortion and wah-wah with heavy blues influences to create his unique style.

This first example, played in the style of "N.I.B.," combines the notes of the E minor scale with a classic bend up to the ♭5th, the blues tritone from the E blues scale.

TRACK 206

This next example showcases Butler's heavy R&B influence. The bass line is played with a shuffle feel and is reminiscent of something he would improvise during an instrumental section in the key of G minor. Everything conforms to a 1–3–1–3 finger pattern, and he sneaks in the blues tritones again by using a third-finger bend.

TRACK 207

FLEA

Bassist Flea from the Red Hot Chili Peppers is one of the more influential contemporary bass players to emerge in the 1990s. Flea earned a reputation for his slapping chops and funk influences, but he's also a master of melodic rock improvisation.

Here's an example in the style of "Dani California" that shows how Flea might play over a simple chord change and add some tasty melodic runs. The progression is a i–VII–iv–i in A minor. Flea plays roots and 5ths below the root for the i and iv chords, while utilizing the A minor pentatonic scale to toss in some melody at the end of each measure. The final bar contains the blues tritone, which is used as a chromatic passing tone.

TRACK 208

Here's a funky bass line in G major that uses the notes of the Mixolydian mode. Flea plays the lower notes on the kick drum to establish the groove and alternately jumps up to the 12th fret to add a few melodic riffs in between.

TRACK 209

Around the time of the *Californication* album, Flea began to write more melodic bass lines that work as a repeated hook during verses or choruses. This next example is in the style of the title track to that album. The progression is a simple i–VI in A minor. On the Am chord, the bass climbs up to the minor 6th and descends back down melodically to the minor 3rd. For the F chord, the F major arpeggio is outlined before descending back down to the same note (C) as in the previous measure.

TRACK 210

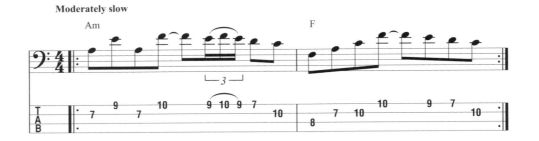

Around the time of the *Stadium Arcadium* album, Flea began using major and minor 10th intervals to bring out some nice melody in the bass. Whereas most bass players would typically play simple octaves on the snare drum hits, Flea opts for these more melodic, wider intervals.

TRACK 211

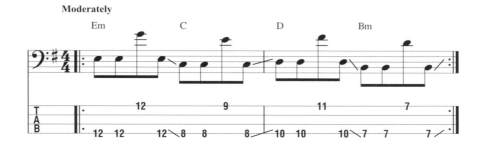

JOHN PAUL JONES

Bassist John Paul Jones of Led Zeppelin was one of the bass greats of the '70s. Influenced by early Motown, blues, and soul, he was a master of groove and improvisation. By taking these elements and applying them to a hard rock and blues context, Jones and drummer John Bonham created one of the most dynamic rock rhythm sections of all time.

This first example is inspired by the chorus section of "Communication Breakdown." The song is in the key of E, with Jones doubling the heavy guitar riff during the verses by using just the root notes, but once the chorus hits, he takes off running on the IV and V chords.

TRACK 212

Notice how the bass utilizes different scales for ascending and descending on each chord. The ascending parts are basically Mixolydian with some additional chromatic passing tones, reinforcing the major or dominant quality of the chords by using the major 3rd and ♭7th. The descending sections use minor pentatonic scales to return the bass to a more classic rock feel. This is a pretty standard move that Jones uses for improvisation throughout the Zeppelin catalogue.

John Paul Jones was also adept at coming up with great melodic bass hooks that breathe life into mellow verses. The next passage is similar to the verse in "Ramble On" and uses the notes of the major pentatonic scale against a simple I–IV chord progression.

TRACK 213

The above example starts out on the tonic (B) and includes a 6th–5th appoggiatura suspension. That melodic phrase is echoed on the IV chord (E) in the second measure before descending down to the 3rd of the chord. In measure 3, the bass jumps up to the 10th to begin a two-measure melodic phrase using the descending B major pentatonic scale.

This next bass line uses the Mixolydian mode and some chromatic passing tones to establish a blues figure in the key of E major. In cases like this, Jones would usually set up a basic motif and use it as a starting point, gradually altering it throughout the song. As with the first example from the previous page, the ascending sections use the notes of the Mixolydian mode, while the descending sections use the minor pentatonic scale.

TRACK 214

PAUL MCCARTNEY

From his work with the Beatles to his band Wings, Paul McCartney is probably the most influential bass player in rock history. His instinct for constructing perfect melodic bass lines has been studied by rock bassists from every generation and genre.

Like the Beatles' music, Sir Paul's bass playing evolved throughout the '60s and continued to do so throughout his years with Wings and his solo career. McCartney is one of the most famous pick players (he started out playing guitar and switched to bass in the very early years of the Beatles out of necessity). Still, he's never played bass like a guitar player, as many guitarists turned bassists do. His bass lines are filled with melody, walking, and groove, all surrounded in a warm, round, thumping tone and a brilliant back beat inspired by the original rock and R&B greats.

As a songwriter, McCartney is a master of melody, and this translates to his bass lines too. He's constantly using scale passages to seamlessly connect the chords in a progression, and will often use inversions, playing the 3rds or 5ths in the bass to achieve a linear, melodic line. McCartney also makes great rhythmic choices to distinguish different sections of songs, to emphasize certain chords within a progression, and to keep the rhythm in between lyrics and vocal phrases flowing and interesting.

This first example illustrates McCartney's great walking instincts and is typical of his playing on the Beatles' early works. It starts off with a continuous scale that descends seamlessly through the first two chords of the progression. From there, it alternates from outlining the arpeggios to simple root–5th patterns. This bass line is similar to the verse in the Beatles' classic "All My Loving."

TRACK 215

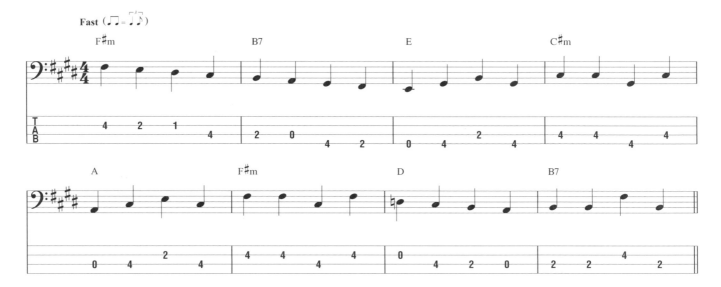

Here's a bass line that's similar to the verse of "You Won't See Me." Here, McCartney establishes a groove and melody by using simple major arpeggios. The pattern is repeated for every chord in this interesting I–II7–IV–I progression.

TRACK 216

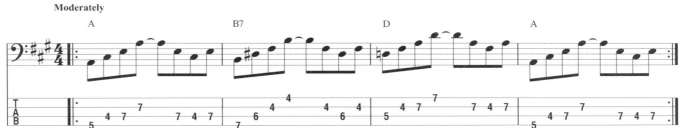

McCartney was also a master of writing great bass parts that would end up becoming the hook of the song. Below is a riff reminiscent of the famous bass part in "Come Together."

TRACK 217

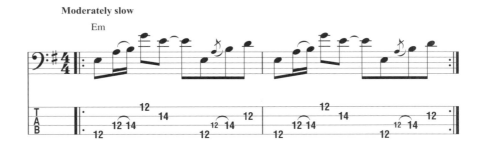

Here's an example that shows how McCartney would often come up with a pentatonic riff and transpose it for each chord of the progression. This approach can be heard in "Day Tripper," "Drive My Car," and "Taxman."

TRACK 218

This next example is reminiscent of the verse from Lennon's "A Day in the Life." McCartney uses chord inversions here to play a smooth, descending bass melody. On beat 3 of the first measure, the bass plays an F#, putting the Bm chord in second inversion. On beat 3 of the third measure, the note B is used as a passing tone, which is actually the major 7th against a C chord. At the end of the second and fourth measures, there's some featured syncopation that occurs right where the vocal rests.

TRACK 219

JOHN ENTWISTLE

The Who's bassist, John Entwistle, had a bright treble tone and an active fingerstyle technique that gave his playing one of the most unique and recognizable bass sounds. His busy, syncopated playing style clashed considerably with drummer Keith Moon's over-the-top theatrical style, yet somehow they came together to create a brilliant and creative rhythm section.

This first example showcases Entwistle's knack for manipulating the pentatonic scale into an effective melody. At first glance, this is simply the descending notes of an A major pentatonic scale, with the chord progression switching between D and A chords. If we take a closer look, though, you can see that Entwistle starts each measure on the note F#, which is the 3rd of the D major chord. In the first and third measures, the bass lands on the root note, A, when the chord changes to A major on beat 3. However, in the second and fourth measures, he employs syncopation, and the bass ends up playing the note C#—the 3rd of the A major chord—when the chord changes.

TRACK 220

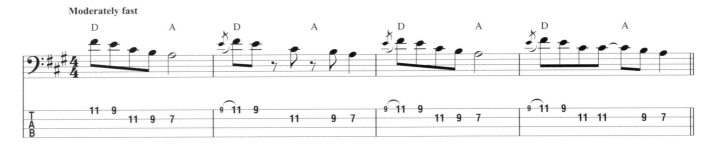

The following example is similar to one of Entwistle's greatest bass lines, featured in the song "The Real Me." The intro and middle sections have minor pentatonic and blues scale solos that span the entire range of the instrument.

TRACK 221

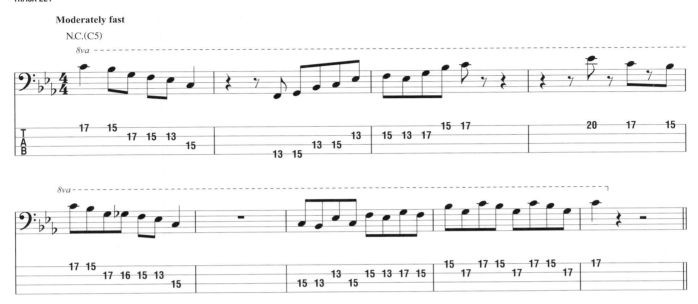

GEDDY LEE

Throughout his four-decade career with Rush, Geddy Lee has attained recognition as arguably the greatest rock bass player of all time. Geddy's style can be broken down into three distinct eras that coincide with the band's evolution, and these periods overlap to great extent. The first era is characterized by epic progressive rock pieces, odd time signatures, long instrumentals, and concept albums like *2112*. This period ends and the next one begins around the time of one of their greatest achievements: the release of their landmark album *Moving Pictures* (1981), which saw the band focused on writing shorter, more commercially accessible songs. The third period began in the '90s, when Geddy changed his right-hand approach to a back-and-forth one-finger technique, simulating a pick player, and the band gradually made their way back to incorporating the epic, progressive roots.

One signature element of Geddy's playing is the use of strategic, quick 16th-note jabs sprinkled within regular eighth-note bass fills, whereby he'll double down on a note in the scale and give it that extra kick. Here's an example of a riff in D major, using the Mixolydian mode, one of Geddy's go-to scales for playing bass fills in major keys.

TRACK 222

Around the time of *Moving Pictures*, guitarist Alex Lifeson began incorporating more and more sus2 chords into the progressions. Geddy addressed these by substituting his octaves with 9ths, and it became one of his great melodic signatures at the time. Bass lines that use this device can be heard in "YYZ" and "The Camera Eye."

TRACK 223

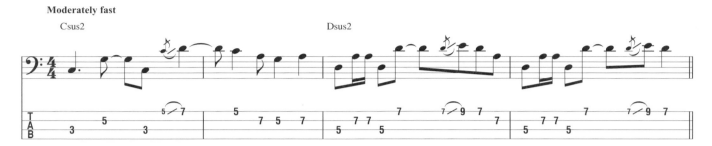

CHRIS SQUIRE

Yes's Chris Squire was one of the quintessential progressive rock bass players. Squire played exclusively with a pick and favored the trebly Rickenbacker sound throughout the '70s. His bass tone has a specific growl to it due to his picking style, whereby he used the edge of his thumb to slightly mute the string while striking it with the pick, giving it a bright yet warm tone. Squire was a master at melody and syncopation, weaving his bass lines seamlessly in and out of odd time signatures. He was also a founding member, songwriter, and priniciple background vocalist in the band, often singing and playing with ease parts that are rhythmically unrelated.

Here's an example of how Squire might use melody and syncopation to connect a chord progression that moves through a few tonal centers. This is similar to some of the bass parts in the song "Starship Trooper."

TRACK 224

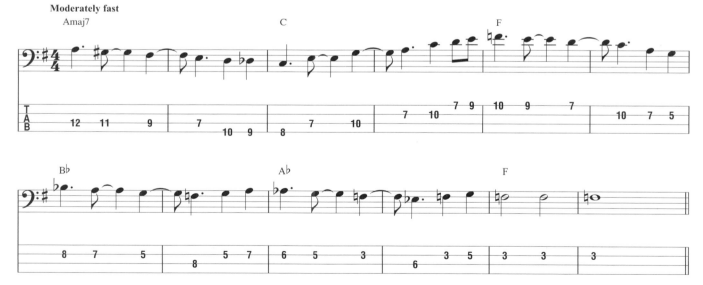

Chapter 16: Play-Along Tracks

The following play-along tracks feature many of the beats and chord progressions used for the examples in this book. Each track contains drums and rhythm guitar, without any bass, giving you space to write, practice, or improvise your own bass lines. When working with these tracks, first determine the beat, key, and chord progression, and then try to apply the many different scales, arpeggios, and techniques covered in the previous chapters. Each example is repeated multiple times, giving you plenty of room to try out different ideas.

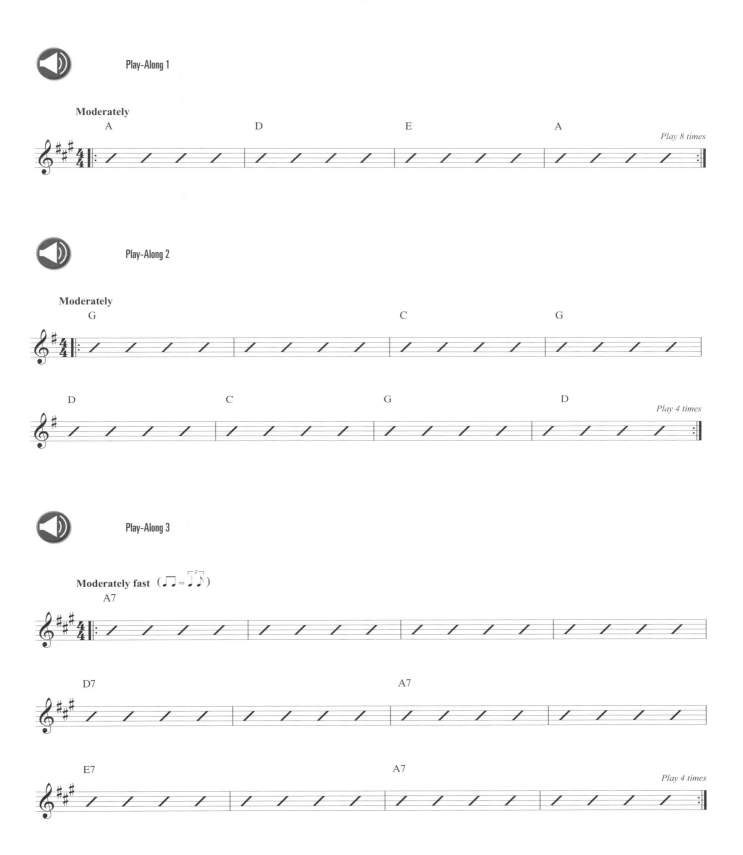

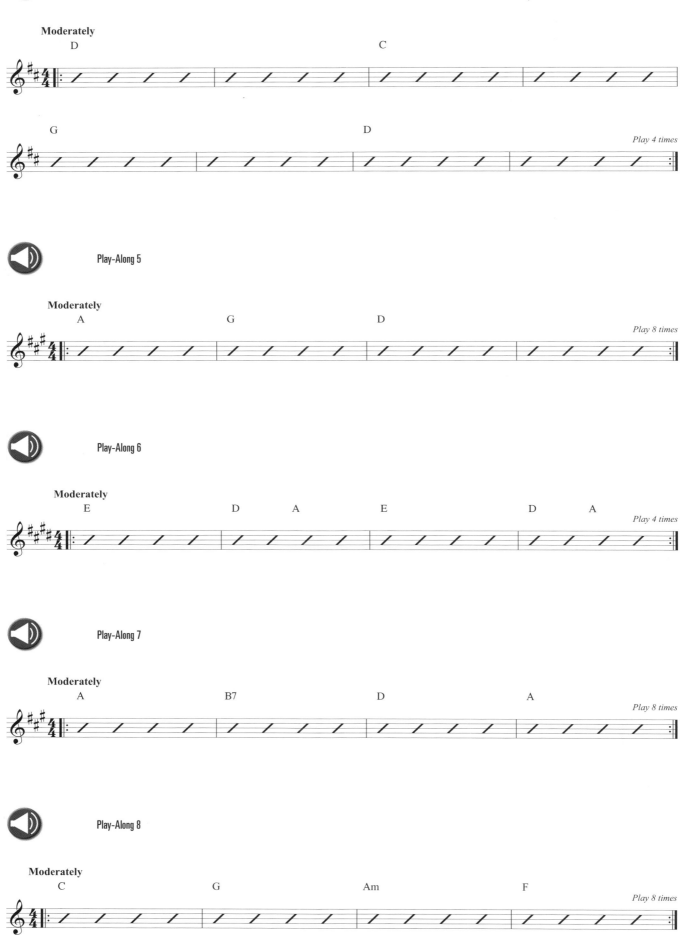

Play-Along 9

Moderately

E D A D E D A D

Play 4 times

Play-Along 10

Moderately

G D Em G D Em

Play 4 times

Play-Along 11

Moderately

Em C D Em

Play 8 times

Play-Along 12

Moderately

Em D C B

Play 8 times

Play-Along 13

Moderately

Em D C B

Play 8 times

Play-Along 14

Moderately

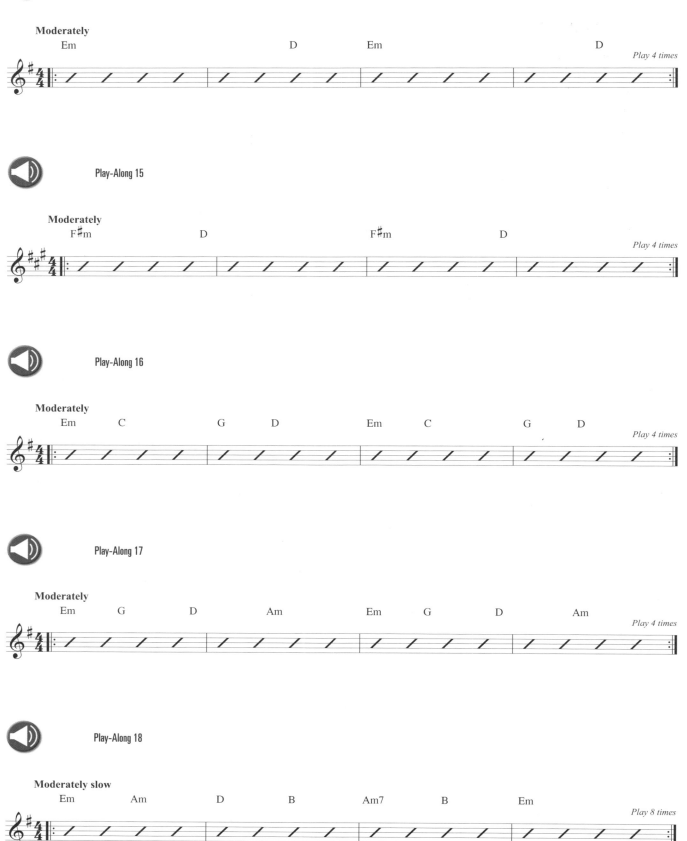

Play-Along 15

Moderately

Play-Along 16

Moderately

Play-Along 17

Moderately

Play-Along 18

Moderately slow

The preceding tracks have all been in common, popular keys, allowing you to try out your ideas in the most familiar keys for bass and guitar. We'd like to encourage you to broaden your horizons and play in keys that may be more suited to keyboards and other instruments. There are many music software programs and apps readily available in which you can easily transpose the rhythm tracks a few steps in either direction, allowing you to practice in closed-position keys such as F, B♭, E♭, and so on. The *Playback+* audio player included with the audio tracks for this book features several great functions for this very purpose: pitch and speed shift, looping, and panning! The more keys you are adept at playing in, the more versatile you'll be as a player. Here are a few examples of rhythm tracks that have been transposed to closed-position keys.

159

BASS BUILDERS

A series of technique book/audio packages created for the purposeful building and development of your chops. Each volume is written by an expert in that particular technique. And with the inclusion of audio, the added dimension of hearing exactly how to play particular grooves and techniques make these truly like private lessons.

BASS AEROBICS
by Jon Liebman
00696437 Book/Online Audio $19.99

**BASS FITNESS –
AN EXERCISING HANDBOOK**
by Josquin des Prés
00660177.. $12.99

BASS FOR BEGINNERS
by Glenn Letsch
00695099 Book/CD Pack...................................... $19.95

BASS GROOVES
by Jon Liebman
00696028 Book/Online Audio $19.99

BASS IMPROVISATION
by Ed Friedland
00695164 Book/Online Audio $19.99

BLUES BASS
by Jon Liebman
00695235 Book/Online Audio $19.99

BUILDING WALKING BASS LINES
by Ed Friedland
00695008 Book/Online Audio $19.99

**RON CARTER –
BUILDING JAZZ BASS LINES**
00841240 Book/Online Audio $19.99

DICTIONARY OF BASS GROOVES
by Sean Malone
00695266 Book/Online Audio $14.95

EXPANDING WALKING BASS LINES
by Ed Friedland
00695026 Book/CD Pack...................................... $19.95

**FINGERBOARD HARMONY
FOR BASS**
by Gary Willis
00695043 Book/Online Audio $17.99

FUNK BASS
by Jon Liebman
00699348 Book/Online Audio $19.99

FUNK/FUSION BASS
by Jon Liebman
00696553 Book/CD Pack...................................... $19.95

HIP-HOP BASS
by Josquin des Prés
00695589 Book/CD Pack...................................... $15.99

JAZZ BASS
by Ed Friedland
00695084 Book/Online Audio $17.99

**JERRY JEMMOTT –
BLUES AND RHYTHM &
BLUES BASS TECHNIQUE**
00695176 Book/CD Pack...................................... $17.95

JUMP 'N' BLUES BASS
by Keith Rosier
00695292 Book/CD Pack...................................... $17.99

**THE LOST ART OF
COUNTRY BASS**
by Keith Rosier
00695107 Book/CD Pack...................................... $19.95

**PENTATONIC SCALES
FOR BASS**
by Ed Friedland
00696224 Book/Online Audio $19.99

REGGAE BASS
by Ed Friedland
00695163 Book/Online Audio $16.95

'70S FUNK & DISCO BASS
by Josquin des Prés
00695614 Book/Online Audio $16.99

**SIMPLIFIED SIGHT-READING
FOR BASS**
by Josquin des Prés
00695085 Book/Online Audio $17.99

6-STRING BASSICS
by David Gross
00695221 Book/Online Audio $14.99

0518